Explore Your Inner Self

BROCKHAMPTON PRESS
LONDON

This edition published 1996 by Brockhampton Press, a member of
the Hodder Headline PLC Group

ISBN 1 86019 380 3

2 4 6 8 10 9 7 5 3

Printed and bound in the UK

Contents

Chapter 1

A State of Confusion

The second part of the twentieth century has seen a great many radical changes, changes that have had a dramatic effect on our way of life. Many of the effects were for the better in that towards the end of the century more people had a comfortable lifestyle than they ever did at the beginning of the century. Some of the effects, however, were not so good. People began to feel stressed and confused, to the extent that they began to question their whole way of life and even their own identity.

'Who exactly am I and why on earth am I doing this?' became a common cri de coeur, if not actually spoken then at least thought. Some who felt a desire to know more about themselves toyed with the idea for a bit, but set it aside and got on with their rat-race lives to the best of their ability. Others again felt that 'Know thyself' was a good maxim for the remainder of their lives and set about putting the knowing of themselves into action.

Exploring one's inner self is obviously no mean task. Even thinking of a way to approach the task is daunting. Different people find different courses of action helpful, and differences in situation can affect the nature of the approach. This book describes some of the ways that people explore in order to get a clearer picture of themselves, but before embarking on such a description it will be helpful to look at the environment that has led so many people to feel a need to search for their own identity and to change their whole way of life in the course of this.

Much of the answer lies in the kind of lives that we have led in the later part of the century. The pace of life and the pace of change were unparalleled, and expressions were coined to reflect these. We had the 'rat race' and we had the 'fast lane', and people got 'burned out' by trying to keep up with the speed of these.

One of the most important changes in the later part of the twentieth century, indeed more a revolution than a change, occurred in the area of technology. The move from work done by men and women to work done by machine began with the Industrial Revolution and climaxed with the New Technology, as the sophisticated technological advances of the late twentieth century have been called.

New technology has affected all of us. Some of the changes that the new automated and computerized systems have brought about have been for the good, some have been for the bad. On the good side, a lot of the drudgery has been taken out of life; on the bad side, many people have lost their jobs. On the good side, a kitchen full of machinery, such as freezers, dishwashers, microwave ovens and food processors, has released the person in charge of family catering to have time to do other things; on the bad side, an office full of computers, word processors and fax machines has vastly reduced the extent and range of job opportunities that offices used to provide for many of the people who were looking for a change from family catering.

Computerization removed not only employment but security. Until it reared what to some is its ugly head, many people left school or university to enter employment that would very likely prove to be a job for life. Some of us enjoy change and like moving from job to job, but others like to find a niche and stay there until retirement age. A classic example of such employment used to be banking, but now rapid automation has drastically reduced a workforce that formerly would have expected to be in safe, secure employment until the end of their working lives.

Historically there was opposition to the Industrial Revolution in the form of the Luddite Riots (1811-12), designed to destroy the machines that were taking away jobs. In modern times people took a long time to appreciate the sheer extent of the change that the new technology would wreak on their lives—what seemed to be in the realms of science fiction one year became actuality the next—and to appreciate just what it would do to employment patterns. In any case, there was little that they could have done to hold back the relentless march of computerization. If the workers had broken up the machines these would have been replaced in no time by even more sophisticated ones, and in the closing decades of the twentieth century people were often too scared of losing their jobs to have taken the kind of industrial action they might have taken earlier in the century. Thus, opposition was not so obvious or so violent at the onset of the new technology as it was during the Industrial Revolution, but its implications were even more far-reaching than those of the Industrial Revolution.

As has already been mentioned, this technological revolution led to a great deal of unemployment, often long-term unemployment, that led to people feeling depressed and unvalued. Also, the unemployment situation was ongoing, a fact that led to people who were in work feeling very insecure, and again unvalued, since they realized that redundancy could strike at any moment and that there were masses of other people on the job market ready to take their jobs if a computer system did not.

Quite suddenly, or so it seemed, the whole basis on which many workers had built their lives, dreams and ambitions, was destroyed. The ground rules had been changed completely, and many simply could not cope with this. Again there was much self-questioning, and even much self-blame, although this was mostly misplaced. There were those whose lives were improved by this self-questioning, since the very act of undertaking it often gave them a greater understanding of their inner selves and a greater realization of what they might do with their lives.

Others simply could not cope with the realization of what had happened to them and tried to behave as though

things were just the same as before—for example, many
men who lost their jobs did not tell their wives or families
but went on leaving home in the morning and returning in
the evening at the same times, just as they had done when
they were working. Some were broken completely, although this very breaking sometimes eventually led to a
self-analysis that led to a greater understanding of themselves and of the opportunities that life still held for them.

It was not only the new technology that caused unemployment and the misery that this engendered. The later
part of the twentieth century has seen times of prosper-
ity—there was, for example, an unbelievable property
boom, and fortunes were made by young people in the
city—but it has also seen times of recession. As employers struggled to balance the books and stay in business,
they shed staff in an effort to reduce their outgoings. The
recession joined the new technology in causing a feeling
of insecurity in those in work and a feeling of despair in
those who were out of work and actively looking for
work. Workers and potential workers all experienced fear
for the future. The 1980s was the decade of the 'yuppy'—
the young upwardly mobile person who reaped significant
financial benefits, but many yuppies were adversely affected by the 1990s.

For various reasons, then, the late 1980s and the 1990s
saw a marked increase in unemployment and a marked reduction in the size of workforces. Because there were
fewer members of staff in the average firm, workers often
found themselves working much longer hours, sometimes

for extra pay, sometimes not. Fear of being sacked or declared redundant made them afraid to refuse to work far beyond their supposed finishing time. This led not only to feelings of tiredness and stress but to feelings of insecurity, and also a sense of being undervalued and of being of no account. Many workers felt that their employers were regarding them not as people but simply as workers who were far from being indispensable. There were plenty more where they came from.

Many employers, even those whose firms were in no danger of going to the wall but simply wanted to maximize their profit margins, did indeed value their employees less and constantly tried to reduce staff levels—by this time the unions were rather a spent force compared with their previous status, and the rights attaching to employment had been reduced or largely ignored by employers. In many cases much of the compassion went out of the employer/employee relationship. If someone was showing signs of stress or of being ill, it was by no means uncommon for employers to take the opportunity to increase the pressure and get the said employee to resign, thereby at the same time reducing the wage budget and obviating any need to provide a redundancy payment.

Lack of compassion became obvious not only between employer and employee but also between employee and employee. The later decades of the twentieth century were decades of materialism and ambition, hence the term, 'rat-race', but by the 1980s, and extending into the 1990s, there was a dog-eat-dog quality about the ambition that set employee against employee. It was not any longer a natural, healthy ambition between colleagues jockeying for promotion. In several offices there was a back-stabbing atmosphere in which people were prepared to go to extraordinary lengths to secure or improve their own position at the expense of that of others. There were even cases of people being afraid to be off ill or to go on holiday in case their jobs were not there when they returned, having been hijacked by colleagues. Far from a feeling of camaraderie among fellow workers, there came into being feelings of suspicion and distrust. Obviously such feelings made the workplace a far from happy one.

Such an employment situation is obviously not good for family life. If spouses and parents are working excessively long hours then obviously they have far less time to spend with their families, and when they do have any time they are likely to be too tired and tetchy to make pleasant companions. Moreover, if they are working in an atmosphere of fear and suspicion they will find it extremely difficult to relax and forget about the work situation when they are at home.

All this has added immeasurably to people's stress levels, stress being very much the designer disease of the late decades of the twentieth century. Anxiety and an inability to switch off from work worries have a very deleterious effect on people's lives and health. Some realize what is happening to them, take a long cool look at themselves and try to get more in touch with their inner selves and their inner desires—this has various results, from a change of career to walking out on wife and family. Others try to soldier on and some become ill, sometimes finding that their illness forces them to take time out of their lives, giving them the time and opportunity to explore their inner selves that they have never had before.

Stress makes it difficult for people to relax, and leisure pursuits are meant to help them do so. The importance of leisure pursuits was much emphasized in the later part of the twentieth century, particularly in the 1970s and the 1980s, and a great boom in the leisure market was forecast and, to a certain extent, was for a time realized. This projected sustained increase in leisure pursuits did not take into consideration the employment situation that was to obtain during recessionary and post-new technology times. People certainly had more leisure, if that is what one cares to call it, but some saw it simply as another euphemism for unemployment. The lack of money that accompanies unemployment meant that many people were not able to take advantage of leisure opportunities, although in some cases these were provided by local authorities, and in some cases unemployed people were able to pay a reduced fee to take advantage of the relevant leisure facility.

Another employment factor has become important in the late twentieth century and has had an effect on family life. The rise of feminism not only gave to women a greater sense of their own worth in what had been a male-dominated world, but it also gave many of them a desire to have a job outside the home and to have a worthwhile ca-

reer. It has been a long struggle, but gradually more employment opportunities have become available to women.
This success, however, has brought about its own stresses.

The work conditions that affect men also affect women.
In terms of sexual equality this is fair enough, particularly
for women who are free of family commitments, but some
women are also mothers. Of course, many men with employment problems are also fathers and theoretically
share the same kind of burden as mothers, but in many instances this burden-sharing stays at the theoretical level.

The last years of the twentieth century have seen the rise
of what is known as New Man, an ideal being who plays
an equal part in the household, doing his share of the
household chores and contributing equally to parenting in
all its facets. Somehow there seem to be very few examples of this ideal being around, outside the features pages
of newspapers, that is. It is a fact that, whether or not the
mother of the family works, the onus of childcare and
housework mostly rests with her.

This, together with difficult employment conditions, im-
poses a weighty burden on working mothers. Reliable
childcare is difficult and expensive to come by, and the
long hours that are expected from employees by employers apply to women as well as men. In some cases the jobs
of women are more taxing, since their very presence in the
workplace is resented by some of their male colleagues.
Many women become exhausted and tense, finding it difficult to cope with the demands of a job, children and a
home when the demands of the job alone are extremely

burdensome. Some of them question whether what they are doing is worth all the effort and trauma. Is the role of superwoman really one that they want to play?

Most of them simply soldier on, primarily because their busy lifestyles leave little time for thought of any kind, let alone thought about what they really want from life. They probably feel that they ought to be more in touch with their inner selves and their inner feelings, but this is put off until another point in their lives when there will be more time—when the children will have left home, for example. Only when something major happens in their lives and they are forced to take life more slowly do they take stock.

A sad fact about life in the later years of the twentieth century is that a great number of people have begun to hate their jobs. Even those who had previously quite enjoyed their actual day-to-day work begin to dislike, and even to dread, going to their place of business every day, partly because of all the politics that go on there, partly because of the level of insecurity and partly because they no longer receive any job satisfaction.

Added to the issues mentioned above is the fact that the average person has become used to a much higher standard of living than was the case in the early part of the century. This has brought with it a marked regard for materialism and a desire for things that cannot really be afforded. Debt has become a way of life, and overdrafts, bank loans and credit cards are part of the average family's budgeting. This is all very well until something goes wrong on the financial front, usually the loss of a job, and unpaid debts begin to pile up. Then a great deal of stress is the result, with a major fear factor being the possible loss of the family home.

All the various areas of stress, including the financial, have a marked adverse effect on marriages and relationships. Many couples cannot cope with the stress and separate or divorce with a consequent effect on any children. Many of these are then brought up by a single parent, usually a single mother, who has to struggle to make ends meet and suffers great stress in the process.

Yet another issue that has added to the complexities and troubles of life in the late twentieth century is the fact that after World War II the population became much more mobile. This mobility of population has continued right into the 1990s, with people leaving the more rural areas where mechanization and other factors have resulted in the reduction of the number of available jobs to go to the cities. Although the intention is to find work, this intention is by no means always realized, and many become homeless as well as jobless and have to resort to living rough on the streets. Young people are the most likely to be mobile, often, for example, leaving home to go to college and settling in other parts of the country or, indeed, the world. Many of them join the ranks of the homeless.

The result of this mobility is that people are no longer as likely to set up home and raise a family near their own parents and members of their close family. The tendency in the early part of the century for members of a family to settle down in the same area as each other, whether this was in a rural or city environment, meant that there was always some kind of ready-made support system for the various members of the family if something went wrong. For example, there was usually a granny or aunt around to take care of the children if the mother was incapacitated or unavailable, as in those pre-feminist days women would have been less likely to be out at work. The net result was that people did not feel so isolated as they sometimes do today. Of course, the various members of the family did not always get on together, but at least they were there for each other in an emergency.

People's sense of isolation could be exacerbated by the fact that the neighbourliness of the early part of the century is not nearly so strong at the end of the century. This is not because people basically became less friendly, although the increased crime rate does tend to make for a greater wariness of strangers and a general tendency to keep one's distance. A much more important factor in the lack of camaraderie among neighbours in the later part of the twentieth century, however, is the fact that everyone has become more and more busy. The pace of life for many people has become such that there is hardly time to smile across the fence at the neighbours, let alone invite them in for coffee or a drink to get to know them.

An added factor, particularly in the 1980s, in the lack of knowledge of one's neighbours was the rate at which people moved house. There was a frenetic quality about the 1980s, and this was particularly well illustrated by the fact that at one point property prices escalated at such a rate that people were moving at an unprecedented rate in order to capitalize on the boom. Prices could quite literally soar from month to month—until the property boom came to an end, seemingly as suddenly as it had begun. This brought further stress, as many families found themselves in a situation of negative equity—with a house the value of which was worth less than the mortgage, even if they could sell it. The ultimate in stress was caused if family members lost their jobs, could not pay the mortgage and had their house repossessed.

This overview of the later years of the twentieth century may seem unnecessarily bleak, and of course those years have had advantages as well as advantages, but the description does serve to emphasize the state that many people are now in. Stress and speed are keynote words, and many feel that they are on a kind of relentless treadmill that it is not possible to jump off. Everything is in a state of hurry and hassle, and there is no time to stand and stare—let alone to think.

In this taut, strained state something has to go. Some people's minds simply cannot take any more, and they have nervous breakdowns. In the case of others, it is their physical health that breaks down. In yet other cases, it proves to be marriages and relationships that cannot stand the strain. In less dramatic cases, some people simply opt out of what they have previously been doing.

People speak of experiencing a personal crisis, a kind of non-age-related extension of what was earlier called a mid-life crisis, a moment of truth when some kind of decision about their lives has to be made. Others speak of requiring space. Many simply want to get off the roundabout of life, which they feel is somehow hurtling round almost out of control, and to stand still for a while.

Certainly the closing years of the twentieth century have found many people feeling lost, as though they have completely strayed from the way on which they had intended to set out. It is a set of circumstances very likely to induce people to try to seek inner strength and inner knowledge in an attempt to improve their lot in some way, and many are doing just that.

It is often something specific that triggers off such a response, some circumstance or life event that makes someone stop in his or her tracks and think. What exactly the crisis point is does, of course, differ from person to person and from circumstance to circumstance.

For some it is the actuality of redundancy. Such an abrupt end to employment naturally distresses, and can even destroy, those to whom it happens. Some people experience a terrible sense of failure and find it difficult, if not impossible, ever to re-establish their self-confidence. Others again, perhaps after an initial feeling of despondency, realize that they are in fact, to their surprise, relieved, even although they may be facing financial hardship.

This sense of relief quite often causes people to stop and wonder why they are experiencing it, and this in turn leads them to try to take a closer look at themselves and to get more in touch with their true feelings. They may begin to question their whole lives so far and to realize that they have been so heavily involved in the rat race that they have never before considered if they had really liked the job they had being doing or from which they had just been sacked.

Many of them come to the conclusion that they would like to do something completely different, and they do so, even at the expense of a huge reduction in their standard of living. They discover a greater gain in personal happiness and contentment, showing that their original misfortune and the consequent chance to contemplate their inner selves have been extremely beneficial.

People who experience this kind of self-appraisal and radical change of lifestyle do not necessarily become declared redundant before they undergo the experience. It can be something that happens at work, perhaps a piece of injustice, perhaps the treachery of a colleague, an excess of stress, perhaps simply the sudden realization of the futility of the job or the lack of job satisfaction. Whatever the actual trigger, the response and result are the same as they are in the case of the people who have been declared redundant.

Sometimes it is a bereavement that triggers the need for self-exploration. For example, a woman who has been widowed and who has never worked outside the home but has spent all her time looking after her husband, her family and the house and garden, might feel completely desolated by his death. She may consider her life rather empty and wonder what to do. It is then that she may well begin to try to get more in touch with herself, to assess what she has accomplished and to try to establish what would really fulfil her. Having explored herself and come to the conclusion that she has unrealized ambitions, she may, for example, start to travel extensively or to embark on a college course of some kind.

People who have suffered from what are known by lay people as nervous breakdowns, or who have suffered from severe reactive clinical depression in response to some form of life crisis, often begin to explore their inner selves as they begin to recover. Having being seriously ill, they often take a new look at life and at themselves, and sometimes alter their entire lifestyles. Those who have been seriously physically ill, such as those who have had a near-death experience during a heart attack, often have a similar response.

It is not always something obviously tragic or unfortunate that leads people to embark on a journey of self-discovery. Sometimes it is a particular age, often the age of forty in men, that triggers it. Sometimes it seems to be nothing in particular that acts as a trigger, just a sudden realization that life is going nowhere and some reappraisal is necessary.

Even a happy event can lead people to try to explore their inner selves. The birth of a baby to a high-powered woman executive might find her suddenly wondering what she really wants out of life and who she really is. Likewise, the marriage of a daughter might find a mother wondering about her role in the family and looking within herself to find out to what extent she has done what she really wanted to do.

The reasons why people embark on a journey of self-discovery are many and varied. The ways in which they set out to explore their inner selves are also many and varied. The following chapters deal with these various ways.

Chapter 2

A Helping Hand

It may seem something of a contradiction in terms to speak of seeking another's help when one sets out to discover one's inner self. Surely only the person involved can bring about such a personal revelation?

To some extent this is true, but some people need a little help, at least to get started on their journey of discovery. Whether or not they do need some assistance will depend partly on the personality of the individual concerned and perhaps partly on the set of the circumstances that led him or her to look at the inner self.

Depression

Some people are already in the hands of other people when they begin to come to terms with their inner selves. We have seen in the previous chapter that what triggers off the need to try to discover oneself can vary a great deal from one person to another, and that there are several possible reasons for setting out on such a journey of revelation. One of these triggering-off points can be an acute mental disorder, such as clinical depression or what is

popularly known as a nervous breakdown, for which
some form of medical treatment is sought.

The nature of the medical treatment will vary according
to the severity of the illness. If, for example, clinical depression is diagnosed early on it can be treated by the patient's general practitioner, but it is the nature of the disorder that, even today, when a great deal more is known
about the condition, it is frequently not identified until it
has become quite severe, when psychiatric treatment and
sometimes hospitalization become necessary.

Drug treatment is often extremely effective in the treatment of clinical depression, and there is a wide range of
these available today. It is recognized, however, that depression is a condition where the person suffering from it
needs to talk to someone, to discuss the life event, such as
bereavement or divorce, that led to the onset of the condition or the set of circumstances that led the person to be a
depressive personality. Psychiatrists are skilled in the art
of drawing people out to talk about themselves and by so
doing can obtain some idea of what has led to their mental
health problems.

In the course of their talks with their psychiatrists, often
when they are in a stage of recovery and so more appre-
ciative of what is going on, patients frequently feel that
they have learned much more about themselves. While
trying to explain their concerns and reactions, and to set
these in the context of the background to their illness, to
the doctors they have given themselves an insight into
their true selves and have a much better picture of what

has made them what they are and what makes them tick.

Several people go on with their self-exploration as a do-it-yourself exercise after having being discharged by their psychiatrists. After they have been shown the way, they feel confident about continuing on their journey of self-discovery on their own. Frequently, self-knowledge acquired in this way leads people to change their lives, or at least to appreciate certain aspects of life more. Some realize, for example, that it was their high-pressure, low-satisfaction jobs that were at the heart of their breakdowns, and they look for a career more in line with what they now see as their true personalities, or indeed decide to opt out of the career structure altogether. Perhaps they are country people at heart, who have been forced to live in a hectic urban environment, and they now revert to type.

It is an unfortunate feature of very severe clinical depression that it can lead to patients suffering from suicidal tendencies. When they have been cured of the feelings of black despair that induces such tendencies, they begin to feel that life is worth living again, and their newly discovered selves begin to think about what is best for them. Nothing much has changed about the world, or about their place in it, but their illness has been a learning experience that has made them see both themselves and the world in a different light.

Psychotherapy
Therapy involving discussion between patient and client need not be organized by a doctor specializing in mental

illness, and the client undergoing the therapy need not be mentally ill. He or she may just feel that there is something wrong with life and be seeking help, or someone who knows the person well may have recommended such a course of action. The person in charge of the therapy programme will not be a psychiatrist but a psychoanalyst or psychotherapist.

A word of warning is necessary here for anyone contemplating this kind of therapy. Psychiatrists are qualified doctors, usually attached to a hospital and people are usually referred to them by a general practitioner. You can have confidence, therefore, in his or her training, even if you do not get on with the actual person. This is not the case, however, with psychotherapists.

Many psychotherapists hold a suitable professional qualification, such as a degree in psychology, and some of them may even be medical doctors, but there is nothing to prevent anyone setting up in business without such qualifications. Some people would argue that it is the skills of the therapist, not the qualifications, that count, but it is as well to check up on the extent of these skills first.

Many general practitioners, conscious of the need for facilities for patients outside mainstream medicine, may make a recommendation. Failing this, do try to get hold of a personal recommendation from someone who has previously attended, and been satisfied with, the psychotherapist—a friend of a friend, perhaps. An attempt has been made to set up a register of therapists, and you could probably obtain details of this from your local public library.

You must feel that you trust the person to whom you are entrusting your mind.

To some extent the skills required by the psychotherapist are those required by the successful psychiatrist. For a start, they must have good listening skills and have the ability to get people to talk about themselves, without revealing any reaction of condemnation or shock. Both need to have skill in interpreting what they hear from the client.

Often the problems that the clients of a psychotherapist have are not too dissimilar from those of the patients of a psychiatrist. Sometimes the difference is only one of degree. For example, two different people might feel that something is not right in their lives and might put this fact down to a bad relationship with a parent—sometimes physical or sexual abuse might be involved—but it is the extent to which this has affected the individual and what he or she decides to do about it that makes the difference.

One may become completely obsessed with the problem—perhaps something like the death of a parent, or even the birth of a son or daughter, might trigger this off. His or her mind ceases to be able to function in the way it normally does, and he or she becomes mentally ill. Medical help has to be sought, and the general practitioner recommends referral to a psychiatrist.

Another person who has much the same problem may not be mentally affected by it to nearly the same extent but may be conscious of the effect it is having on his or her life—perhaps he or she is having difficulties in forming lasting relationships. The person realizes that help must be sought and thinks of psychotherapy. Perhaps he or she may have a friend who has undergone such treatment and may be able to recommend a psychotherapist.

The basis of modern psychoanalysis and psychotherapy goes back to the Austrian psychiatrist Sigmund Freud, the inventor of psychoanalysis. The disciplines seek to tap into the subconscious of the individual undergoing analysis or therapy and to release any hidden fears and to unblock any repressed emotions. By this means, people seek to find out more about their true selves.

The major difference between psychoanalysis and psychotherapy is that, as the name suggests, the latter seeks to heal. The suppressed fears and emotions that emerge from analysis are not an end in themselves but a means by which the healing process may be begun. By unblocking the subconscious, the therapist tries to help the client towards a better understanding of himself or herself and to help him or her to cope more effectively with life in the light of this understanding.

The role of the psychotherapist is to listen and interpret what the client is saying. Some people feel that simply talking to someone who is a complete stranger is in fact therapeutic. Friends and members of the family may be too involved, over-emotional, or even condemnatory or judgmental, and furthermore be always too busy really to listen. The psychotherapist is someone who is totally uninvolved and detached, whose good opinion or otherwise does not matter, and who has the time to listen. Furthermore, and this is an important part of psychotherapy, the talking can go on over a longish period of time, often quite a few months, so that there is no sense of rush. There is plenty of time to explore past experiences and relationships. The person with a problem feels that at last there is someone there to listen and help.

The basic aim of analysis and therapy may not vary from one psychotherapist to another, but the method of approach does. Some of them are closer to the techniques of Freud than others and advocate that clients say anything that comes into their heads, using a kind of free association as a means of unblocking the unconscious. Other therapists may prompt the client with a few gentle leading questions, especially as a means of getting each session started.

Some adopt a more formal, traditional approach than others and have the client lying on a sofa in such a way that he or she is unable to see the therapist. External stimuli are reduced to a minimum in an effort to get the client to concentrate as much as possible on his or her own thoughts. Others regard this, which is very much the usual public perception of the office of a psychotherapist or of a psychiatrist, as being too rigid an approach and choose to talk to their clients in a less formal setting, although the therapists themselves are never intrusive.

Many people find psychotherapy a very useful and rewarding step on their way to self-discovery. At the very least they have talked about things that they would never have dreamt of speaking about before and have learned to face up to them. They have been helped to come to terms

with the past and have been able to achieve some understanding of how the past, with its suppressed fears and
emotions, had affected the present and prevented them
living life to the full. In a very real sense, many people
discover who they really are through psychotherapy. Now
they are ready to build a future.

There are some who see drawbacks in psychotherapy.
The process of psychotherapy, as we have seen, aims to
release blocked and negative emotions by getting clients
to talk about things that had happened in their lives but
had been subconsciously blocked out by them. Some
sceptics are afraid that some of the psychotherapists' clients are talking not only about terrible things that had happened in their lives but about terrible things that had not
happened at all but are the products of the clients' imagi-
nation.

This phenomenon, the existence of which is denied by
many, is known as 'false memory'. Cited examples of it
include people who suddenly claim that they were abused
in some way, often sexually abused, when this seems
highly unlikely in the light of evidence put forward by
parents, other family members, neighbours, and so on.
There are stories of parents being completely rejected by
their grown-up children after therapy, when previously
they had seemed to enjoy a very happy relationship—although it has to be borne in mind that only two people
need to know the truth about abuse, onlookers being often
ignorant of the truth.

Not enough is yet known about 'false memory', although the argument about it rages on. What is the case is that more and more people are turning to psychotherapy. People nowadays are considerably better informed, and they have a much better idea of when to seek help and where to find it. Many know the importance of being put in touch with themselves and with their own feelings, and many choose to do so by means of psychotherapy.

Counselling

If people have a particular problem that is having a harmful effect on their lives, they may care to seek help not from a psychiatrist or a psychotherapist but from a counsellor. Counselling has become a very important part of our lives in the late twentieth century, although it is quite a recent phenomenon.

Counselling tends to seek to help someone deal with a particular experience rather than delve into the subconscious, as psychotherapy does, but the simple fact of talking to someone about a specific problem can have a wider therapeutic effect. We have become increasingly aware of the trauma, both long-term and short-term, that can be caused by some life events, and counselling is very often recommended to someone who has just experienced such an event.

Psychotherapy plays a more obvious role in a journey of self-discovery than counselling does. Events that interrupt the smooth progress of our lives, however, such as the traumatic events that lead to the necessity for counselling, tend to pull us up short and make us start thinking more about who we are and where we are at. In addition, talking about a problem to someone and working our way through it can make us start thinking more closely about our emotions and thoughts generally. The net result is often that we find we have gone through a learning experience that has left us wanting to know more about ourselves.

There is a wide range of life events in which counselling is appropriate. For example, someone who has been involved in some terrible car accident in which others have been killed may well be advised to seek counselling. Likewise, someone who has just given birth to a stillborn child and is having difficulty in coming to terms with the situation may be advised to seek counselling to try to deal with the potential long-term effects of such bereavement.

Public bodies are also becoming aware of the need for counselling for people who have come through traumatic situations. Before, it was assumed that it was part of the job, and people were told to pull themselves together and get on with their lives. Now, for example, police officers who have watched a colleague being shot to death, or a firefighter who has failed to rescue a child from a blazing building, may well be offered counselling, and it has been suggested that this also be offered to soldiers who have experienced trauma in battle. People who undergo trauma and who do not receive counselling are thought to be in danger of what is known as post-traumatic stress syndrome or disorder.

Schools often offer counselling to schoolchildren if one of their number is suddenly killed. Perhaps the death was the result of some terrible accident; perhaps the child met a violent death by murder. Whatever the cause of death, it is recognized now that the other children in the school need to be able to grieve and so are offered counselling to try to obviate any ill effects on them in a later life.

When someone seeks counselling about a problem, he or she will be put in touch with someone who will discuss the situation from a sympathetic point of view and often offer practical advice. Frequently the object of counselling is to talk through the problem in such a way that the discussion will enable the person seeking counselling to discover for himself or herself the solution to the problem. It is often this working-through process that puts the person concerned in control of his or her own life again.

There are some extremely effective counsellors around, some of them attached to a particular body or organization. As is the case with psychotherapists, however, there are some counsellors practising who have minimal skills and minimum training, partly because it very rapidly became rather a trendy profession with no very obvious basic qualifications. Again it is wise to seek guidance from your general practitioner or hospital, or from a friend with some experience of the field of counselling.

Hypnotherapy

Some people, in an effort to help them sort out their problems, turn to a hypnotherapist. These problems range from trying to break an addiction, such as smoking, to trying to slim by receiving help in controlling the appetite, from trying to increase one's level of confidence, to trying not to be so self-conscious, or to trying to help solve some emotional problems.

Hypnotherapy often receives a bad press. It is frequently associated in people's minds with stage or television shows where people are sometimes made to look extremely foolish when hypnotized. The impression created is that the subject, usually someone from the audience who has been foolish enough to volunteer, is completely under the control of the hypnotist. Lots of stories, many of them doubtless apocryphal, circulate about how people injured themselves or were even killed or died while under hypnosis.

There may be a few charlatans in hypnosis, but then so there are in most areas of life, including therapy and healing. There are a great many skilled hypnotists as well, however, using their skills for therapeutic purposes, and many members of the medical and dental professions recognize that hypnosis can play an important role in mental and physical health.

Many people think that when one is in a hypnotic state one is actually asleep, but this is not the case. Hypnosis is not sleep. It is more a state where one withdraws from the normal state of consciousness but yet does not reach the unconscious state. It is like a borderline state between consciousness and unconsciousness, which acts as a link between the two states. When in a hypnotic state, one remains, to some extent, aware and deeply absorbed but is open to hypnotic suggestion.

Some people are easier to put under hypnosis than others. It is quite important that the intended subject has some belief in hypnosis, and is prepared to let go and be totally relaxed. The person bringing about a hypnotic state in someone usually adopts a fairly unobtrusive manner and a quiet, monotonous tone of voice. He or she frequently fixes the person about to be hypnotized with a steady, fixed gaze and sometimes holds an object slightly above the person's eye-level and moves it regularly from side to side. Some hypnotists will say something along the lines of 'Your eyelids are getting heavy. Your eyes are beginning to tire. You can hardly keep your eyes open.' In fact the person's eyes are likely to feel tired, not only from hypnotic suggestion but also because of constantly directing the eyes upwards at the moving object.

We have seen how hypnotherapy can be used in several ways, such as helping people to stop smoking. Hypnosis can, however, be used specifically to get us to be more in touch with ourselves. Sometimes called hypnoanalysis in this context, it was used by Freud before he went on to practise psychoanalysis. By means of hypnotic suggestion, the person seeking help through hypnosis can move backwards in time, in a kind of regression, and relive memories that would not be recoverable by ordinary memory or an act of will. This can add to our self-knowledge in somewhat the same way that psychoanalysis can, although many people would prefer psychoanalysis or psychotherapy to hypnoanalysis since they feel, although this might not necessarily be the case, that they are more in control. There is sometimes a vague feeling among people in general that to undergo hypnosis is to put oneself entirely in someone else's power, although this is not in fact true.

There is another way that hypnosis can help us on our journey of self-discovery. It has been pointed out above that hypnosis is sometimes recommended as a possible cure for some kinds of addiction, as in tobacco addiction or food addiction. If cure by hypnosis is effective in cases of addiction, it helps to put the addict back in charge of his or her life instead of being under the control of the addictive substance. As will be discussed later in the chapter, under the heading of Addiction with relation to self-help groups, addiction often results in alienation from one's self. By the same token, breaking free from addiction frees the self and is instrumental in allowing former addicts to get to know their real selves.

As is the case if you are seeking a psychotherapist, you should be very careful when seeking out a hypnotist, simply because of the difficulty of imposing a standard of training and skill in such a discipline. Again it is worth starting with your general practitioner or your local health centre, or perhaps with a friend who has undergone hypnosis and found it useful. There are some people who have mastered the art of self-hypnosis, but it is important to seek professional advice and to do quite a lot of research on the subject before you actually try this. You do not want to become involved in something that you find you cannot handle.

Self-help groups for addicts

This chapter is dealing with people who can help others on a journey of self-discovery, usually by helping them cope with some problem or disorder that is having an effect on their lives. It may seem like a contradiction in terms, therefore, to mention self-help groups, such groups being a set of people who have the same kind of problem and who meet together to work through this, and to offer advice and support to each other. I have included the groups in this chapter, simply because, as is the case with counselling, someone has to point the person seeking help in the right direction, and the other members of the group have to give any new member a great deal of support. Only then can he or she learn to begin to cope with the problem involved and begin to contribute effectively within the group.

The first self-help groups began in the United States in the 1930s to help people suffering from alcoholism to cure themselves. Alcoholics Anonymous was the first well-known self-help group, and it is probably still the best known. They hold regular meetings to help members face up to their drink problem, to help them break the habit, and to help them fight the temptation to start again. The meetings provide a forum where you can share your problem with others, knowing that they too have first-hand experience of the problem. People who are trying to break free of their addiction know that they are in no danger of being patronized by do-gooders or of being in receipt of contempt or condemnation. They are among their own.

A similar group is Gamblers' Anonymous, which provides the help for those addicted to gambling that Alcoholics Anonymous does for those addicted to alcohol. The extent of gambling addiction in this country has increased greatly in recent years, partly because the potential for gambling has increased so much. Formerly it was only betting on horses that was the problem, but there is concern, particularly with reference to the young, about addiction to fruit machines, and now there are worries that the National Lottery, particularly in its scratch card versions, will add to gambling tendencies, especially in people who are too poor to indulge such tendencies with equanimity. Those of us who buy the occasional lottery ticket have no idea of the forces that are at work in someone spending the week's housekeeping on scratch cards. It is all too easy to condemn without appreciating the problem. At Gamblers' Anonymous this ready condemnation is unheard of.

Self-help groups for those with some form of addiction are extremely important because they not only help addicts to keep away from their particular form of addiction but they also help them to rebuild their lives and give them back their self-esteem and self-control. Addicts are never in control of their own lives until they can relinquish their addiction, because to be addicted to something is to be controlled by it. Thus it is that alcohol, gambling, or whatever form the addiction takes, rules the addicts, and they themselves are virtually powerless.

The source of the addiction alienates addicts from their

true selves. While they are in its grip they cannot really know themselves, as their true selves have become submerged and subjugated. Coming to terms with addiction and ceasing to be the slave of the addictive substance means that the former addicts can come terms with themselves and embark on what is a very important journey of self-discovery, to find the lost self.

The self-help groups for addicts that have so far been mentioned have been large groups designed either for people suffering from alcohol abuse or from gambling addiction. There are, of course, other addictions—one very obvious and very serious one being that of drug abuse—and there are self-help groups for some of these, some local groups and some branches of larger groups.

Addicts need all the help they can get, although of course they first have to want to break free from the addiction. It is frequently maintained that addicts are never really cured, that the most that they can hope for is that they will stay away from the addictive substance or habit, although that is in fact a major achievement. Being able not actually to involve themselves with the addiction to a large extent puts them in charge of themselves again, although many of them need the support of the self-help group for life.

Self-help groups for non-addicts

Self-help groups do not exist simply for addicts. They have proved of enormous help to many others and deal with a wide range of problems or experiences. For example, parents whose children have been the victims of cot death often find great comfort from being with people who have been in the same terrible situation. They realize that they are not alone and that they are in no way to blame for the tragedy, although some of them will have been torturing themselves with this thought.

Another well-known self-help group is Al-Anon, which provides help and understanding for the members of the family of someone who is suffering from alcohol abuse. This is a particularly useful group since alcohol destroys not only individuals but whole families, coming, as it often does, accompanied by violence, poverty and loss of self-esteem. Often family members feel, usually quite wrongly, a sense of blame and a sense of failure if they have been unable to get the alcoholic to stop drinking.

Other self-help groups include those formed by people who have been raped; those formed by people who have suffered sexual abuse; those formed by people who are suffering from Aids or who are HIV-positive; those formed by people who are part of the adoption triangle, whether they be adopts, adoptive parents, or birth parents who gave their children up for adoption; those formed by people who suffer from depression; the list is practically endless. Obviously, the nature of the groups will vary one from another, but they have in common the fact that the members all know what other members are going through, and they know exactly what to do to help. Being part of a group takes away the terrible sense of isolation that is often felt by people who are suffering in some way.

'Why me?' they often ask, and it is something of a comfort that God or fate has not selected them alone to undergo tragedy or disorder.

We have seen how self-help groups for people fighting an addiction can help the members lose their sense of alienation from themselves and discover more about themselves while helping them to fight the addiction. Members of other groups will not necessarily have suffered a sense of alienation from themselves, but whatever traumatic experience it is that they are recovering from will have left its mark. This tragic learning experience will have stopped them in their tracks, but the help and support that they receive from fellow group members will enable them to recover enough from the trauma to be able to stop and think, and to use the learning experience in a positive way so that it may well in some way enrich their lives. The whole experience will certainly tell them a good deal about themselves, their strengths and weaknesses, and will be a major stage in any journey of self-discovery.

Women's self-help groups
There are some organizations that aim to encourage self-help among women with particular needs. Such organizations, of which Women's Aid is a well-known example, provide refuges for battered wives and encourage the women to take charge of their lives. The location of the refuges is kept strictly secret so that husbands who have acted violently towards their wives will not be able to track them down and attempt to take them back.

As has been indicated, the aim of these women's organizations is to get women who have suffered at the hands of violent partners to take charge of their own lives and to try to make new and independent lives for themselves away from the tyranny of violence. To some extent, however, the self-help is the second part of this aim. First the women have to feel assured that there is somewhere safe to go before they take the huge step of leaving their home and partner. Organizations like Women's Aid, with their refuges and staff providing backup support and advice on benefits, childcare, job opportunities and many other areas of concern, provide such assurance.

Women, particularly women with children, never leave violent partners lightly. Most of them keep hoping for some form of miraculous change in the man concerned, who may be very charming when he is not in the grip of violence. When they eventually face the fact that this is not going to happen, when they start to become terrified for their children as well as for themselves, indeed when they begin to fear for their very lives, they often still hesitate before leaving, even if they know about the work of the women's organizations and the refuges.

The recurrent violence, which will often have been accompanied by verbal abuse, will very likely have left the women with very low self-esteem. They have probably been told repeatedly that they are useless, and they have begun to believe what has been said. Worse, they frequently feel that they are responsible for what is happening to them. A woman may feel that if her partner is so charming to everyone else then it must be something in her that is inviting the blows.

A woman who leaves her partner and then returns to him feels even less self-esteem, since she has tried and failed. The failure may well have been no fault of her own, but she will not see it that way. Many battered women go to their parents or other family members and return because the partner turned up at their house, made a scene and offered violence to her family. They sometimes return because their families do not have the space to accommodate her and the children, or the money to support them, or sometimes are not willing to offer them either financial or emotional support. Sadly, they frequently return when their violent partners tell them that they will take the children from them if they do not return.

The woman who has heard about one of the agencies that help battered wives—such agencies, fortunately, are now much better known than they were formerly—and decides that there is no hope other than to leave and seek their help, has already embarked on a journey of self-discovery as well as one of self-help. When she leaves she realizes that she has more strength than she thought she had—the sheer act of leaving is testament to this. After she has received help and advice she will realize that she has far greater potential than she felt she ever had before, and this will in turn lead to greater self-confidence. When she has been out on her own for a bit, and coping with children and home on her own, she may well begin to take stock and really begin to discover even greater depths in herself.

For some women their new-found liberation from violence and their new independence will have been part of a
journey of self-discovery, but for others they may be a
part of a journey of rediscovery. They may have been
quite different people, when they married, from the fright-
ened, shivering, worthless-feeling wrecks that they became. The incidence of domestic violence is not related to
class, education or money, and some women might have
had quite good jobs before marrying jealous men and giving up their jobs. As she re-establishes her life independ-
ently of her violent husband she will probably also end up
on a journey of discovery as she reflects on how far she
can come and on how far she can go.

Thus we have seen how some people who have been rendered vulnerable in some way, or who have suffered some
form of trauma, can achieve some degree of self-discovery in the course of seeking help with their problems.

There can be benefits from the experience of trauma, and
these benefits are enhanced by the help given in the various ways described above. Thus psychiatry, psychotherapy, counselling and self-help groups can not only
help people towards a greater sense of wellbeing and a
greater sense of being at peace with themselves, but they
can also help them to have a greater understanding of their
inner selves.

Traditional methods of help—religion
In a way, the professionals involved in the processes described in this chapter so far are the priests of the modern

world. In earlier centuries, or even in the earlier decades of the twentieth century, people with some of the problems described above would seek the help of a priest or minister of the church. Particularly in the second part of the twentieth century, however, the number of people taking part in organized traditional religions diminished considerably, and so this no longer became an option for them.

Of course the priest or minister would not have the range of professional expertise of some of today's advisers, but in earlier times, including in the earlier decades of the twentieth century—the infancy of psychiatry—the kind of trauma and the kind of emotional problems that are now generally acknowledged as affecting the lives of people were simply not known or not recognized as such. Problems were seen in more simplistic terms, and members of the clergy were expected to be able to deal with these.

Things were often seen in moral or ethical terms, and clergymen were judged to be eminently qualified to deal with such issues. Spiritual issues, such as crises of faith, were obviously also adjudged to be part of their remit, and many more issues than were strictly relevant to the spiritual topic were included under its umbrella. There may well have been objections to this kind of blanket coverage of problems by the clergy, but there was little alternative.

At least in the case of families whose members had tended to stay much in the same place for some time, the relevant clergymen had a background to go on when offering advice. He probably had a very real idea of the weaknesses and strengths of the various family members, and this might well have proved useful when trying to show someone the way forward to a greater contact with his or her inner self. No one exists in a vacuum, and the past often has a very powerful influence on the present and even on the future.

So much for the influence of the clergy on the family, which in time waned dramatically as it became no longer the norm in Britain for people to attend church regularly, whether or not they were members of the Church of England, the Roman Catholic Church, the Church of Scotland, the Methodist Church, the Baptist Church or any of the others. There are still some people who do not attend church regularly but who still opt to get married, to be buried and to have their children baptised under the auspices of the church—some may even feel a nostalgic desire to attend church at Christmas and Easter.

On the other hand, secular arrangements for the major events in life are becoming more and more common in Britain all the time. More and more people are choosing to be married in registry offices, and efforts are being made to make civil wedding ceremonies more civilized, welcoming and considerably less bleak. In any case, more and more couples are opting to live together instead of getting married, some for part of the time that they are together, some for all of the time that they are together, even after they have children. The net result is that many couples are relinquishing even the tenuous connection that they had with the church, although there still exist brides who think that a church is a better backdrop for their wedding photographs than a registry office and who will spend quite a time looking for a particularly pretty church to serve the purpose.

Even people who declared themselves to be agnostics or even atheists in life used to be buried under the auspices of the church. In recent years, it has become common for the burial service to be a cremation service, churchyards and cemeteries being no longer able to cope with the sheer volume of corpses and cremation becoming a more compact acceptable alternative. For a long time the cremation ceremony was still very much a 'service'. Although the ceremony would take place in a crematorium rather than a church, the person who usually officiated at such a ceremony was a minister or priest of the church.

Gradually the secular impression created by the often rather bleak crematorium got people used to dissociating the idea of interment and the church. Frequently the relatives of the person being cremated had to make a lot of enquiries in order to find a minister or priest to officiate, and even then the cleric had a great deal of difficulty finding something complimentary and truthful about someone whom he or she had hardly known—if at all.

Many people began to feel that the whole thing was becoming a bit hypocritical and sought to make the whole cremation ceremony more secular. This has become particularly easy to organize if the person who has died was a member of the Humanist Society, as they will provide for someone to officiate at a secular ceremony.

For many, the church baptismal service has long been
something that deviates from the truth. Either godparents
or parents, or both, are required to promise to bring the
child up according to the dictates of the church and to be
responsible for his or her spiritual and moral welfare. This
many of them have done—and never been near a church
after the baptismal service or seen to it that the child has.
Gradually the secularization of marriage and burial ceremonies has spilled over into baptismal ceremonies. Formerly, there was a general feeling that children were not
quite legally registered if they were not baptised in
church, there being some confusion between civil registration of the birth, compulsory by law, at the local registry office, and baptism in church. In time more people became aware that the civil registration was enough.

Certainly, by the very late decades of the twentieth century, the church had ceased to play a major part in many
people's lives. If births, marriages and deaths could be officially recognized without benefit of clergy then many
people had little use for the church. Of course this is by
way of being a generalization. Many people, particularly
those of an older generation, have gone on attending
church regularly, and some others have gone on paying
lip-service to the church by using it for family marriages,
births and deaths, and perhaps have graced it occasionally
at Christmas and Easter. Another point worth making is
that many of the churches have tried valiantly to modern-
ize themselves, indeed have even made themselves
trendy, in an effort to attract more people, particularly

younger people, back to the church. Alas, in many cases the effort has not been totally successful. Perhaps one could say in all charity that the efforts were a classic case of too little, too late.

What has been missing for some considerable time is the emphasis placed on pastoral care by the clergy in the average community. Many families would feel extremely embarrassed, and even encroached upon, if a member of the clergy called, even if the family was going through a bereavement or other family crisis, and even if its members were still technically members of the church. On the other side of the clerical fence, so to speak, the clergy, although coping with fewer church members, are probably also trying to cope with larger workloads, fewer clerical colleagues and an ageing church membership, which makes more demands on their time, not least in terms of bereavement. They may have very little time to experience the embarrassment they might encounter if they enter a house of church membership, but not of churchgoers, or even a house of agnostics or atheists that happens to be situated in their parish.

This represents a complete turnaround. There was a time in the relatively recent past when pastoral care was of major importance in the community. If something major went wrong in the life of a member of the family, the local minister or priest was likely to be among the first to be consulted. Thus, if a husband died, or a child was stillborn, or a daughter became pregnant while unmarried, or a son ran away from home, then both spiritual comfort and practical help would be sought from the relevant local cleric. Before the advent of a higher general standard of education and while literacy levels were quite low, the local clergyman was also the person to whom people turned if some kind of official letter had to be written or even read.

The standing of the clergy in the average community has fallen drastically, although the extent of this falling-off has obviously differed from church to church, area to area, and even person to person. With this reduction of importance of church and clergy in the average family's life has come an inevitable decrease in pastoral care. When the family members could no longer turn to the parish minister or priest for help or comfort, then they had to look elsewhere—to psychotherapists, counsellors and self-help groups in fact.

The fact that a great many people have abandoned the church as a source of solace, and even of self-discovery, does not mean that this is true for everyone. There is still a significant number of people in Britain who are staunch members of the church and who regard religion as a spiritual quest and thus a journey of self-discovery.

Furthermore, there are many people who were not brought up in the ways of organized religion but who seek membership of a church to help them find a faith, often in an attempt to help them find themselves, or at least to help them come to terms with themselves. Some of these speak of suddenly seeing the light, as though their lives up to the point of their conversion to religion had been deep in darkness. Such people may be seen as being against the trend, but there are others who, to some extent, might be seen in the same context.

These include people who, in their early years, were brought up to be regular churchgoers and believers in religion but who somehow let such habits and such beliefs lapse, only to find that at the point of some crisis in their lives they felt a need to revert to these and began to attend church regularly, and to consult priests and ministers of religion. They frequently feel that they have somehow lost themselves along life's way and have a deep conviction that the only way to get back in touch with themselves is through the church. Some of these turn to a church other than the one in which they were brought up. For example, a member of the Church of England might feel that he or she wishes to join the Roman Catholic Church.

Often people who either join the church or revert to regular churchgoing are seeking help, sometimes consciously, sometimes unconsciously, with a problem, whether this be an emotional, mental or spiritual one. Whatever the problem, they are probably also seeking to find spiritual enlightenment or fulfilment, and by so doing to extend their knowledge of themselves.

They see their parish minister or priest as a source of help, support and enlightenment, someone to whom they can entrust their deepest thoughts and feelings without fear of these being passed on without consultation. Often by talking these through with the cleric, the problem-ridden people can find their own answers to what is bothering them, while at the same time adding a spiritual dimension to their lives that enriches and extends them.

This is all very well for people who have a religious faith or for people who are working their way towards a religious faith. They have someone trustworthy on hand to whom they can confide their innermost secrets and thoughts, and by so doing they can explore their inner selves. People without religious faith and without a church connection do not have such an outlet. That is why they seek help from other sources, which take on the mantle of a religious confessor and confidant and which can help them on their path to greater self-knowledge. Thus the need for psychotherapists, counsellors and self-help groups.

In our multicultural society it is not uncommon for people to seek solace in one of the eastern religions, although they were not born into one of these. At school many people learn something about other religions as well as Christianity, and some feel drawn to these. The eastern influence on some people's religious feelings was very prominent in the 1960s, when a good many people, particularly young people, went off to India in search of spiritual fulfilment and often in search of a guru, a spiritual teacher, who would bring them such fulfilment. The guru took the place that a clergyman would once have held in their lives but had the advantage of being considerably more exotic in their eyes. This trend towards eastern religions was increased by the interest of the Beatles, the British pop group that leapt to extraordinary fame in the 1960s. John Lennon in particular was drawn towards the East and influenced other young people.

For many young people the looking towards the east for spiritual satisfaction was an attempt to get in touch with their inner selves, the guru being a guide to show the way. It was also an attempt to give expression to their dissatisfaction with the materialistic way of life of the West, often the way of life of their middle-class or upper-class relatives. This dissatisfaction was also displayed by people who embraced the Hippie culture in the 1960s and later by people who embraced the New Age philosophy in the late 1980s and 1990s. These movements are treated in greater detail in the next chapter.

Of course not everyone who felt drawn towards the religions and philosophies of the East went to India in search of a guru—neither did they all seek out one of the gurus who came to the West. Indeed, many more people than embraced the whole panoply of a religion such as Hinduism or Buddhism simply adopted parts of these. Thus they came to be drawn towards meditation and yoga, and these activities often took the place that Christian prayer would once have done in their lives.

As has been mentioned, many people in the 1960s felt drawn to gurus in the hope that they would give them spiritual leadership and help them to a greater realization of their inner selves. Later in the twentieth century there was an increased tendency for people to join religious cults and to look towards the cult leader for the same kind of guidance that some had looked for in gurus in the 1960s, and countless others had looked for in clergymen throughout the centuries. Cult members were often looking for some kind of inner fulfilment or realization and looked to the cult leader to help them in their journey towards this. Religious cults were more common in the United States than in Britain, but in both countries fears were expressed that members of the cults were being brainwashed, although there is often a danger that someone vulnerable, seeking emotional or spiritual help, will form too great an attachment to the person seeking to provide such help.

There is a very real need in many of us to find spiritual fulfilment, whether or not we would categorize the need as such, and in order to do this we often feel that we have to find ourselves or to reach a clearer understanding of ourselves. This often involves seeking help from someone professionally concerned in some way with this kind of work, and such a person is personally central to the success of the other person's search for self. Such help has been described in this chapter, but there is also help to be provided in a less central, more peripheral way, by other people. This kind of help, together with the kind of help that people embarking on a journey of self-discovery might provide for themselves, is described in the next chapter.

Chapter 3

Self-Help

The previous chapter deals with situations in which other people, at least at first, play a major part in our attempts to seek out our inner selves. This chapter explores the attempts made by people themselves to undertake a journey of self-discovery. Although again they may receive help and encouragement from other people, the other people do not play such a major role as, for example, a psychotherapist.

There are many different ways in which people seek to become more in touch with themselves and to find out more about themselves. Some people find a method that suits them right away, although the actual self-exploration might take a considerable time. Others try various methods before hitting on the one that contributes to their self-discovery.

Solitary self-exploration
Some seek solitude in which to create the right kind of atmosphere for communing with themselves. This can be quite informal and might take the form of a quiet holiday

in which the person on a journey of self-exploration goes off alone, often somewhere solitary, such as a remote cottage, to find time and space to think and reflect, and to provide an opportunity for self-analysis. People who opt out of their usual worlds in this way, whether for a short or long time, often do so to give themselves the opportunity to look at their lives and to consider the past, present and what seems to be the likely future. Some go back refreshed by such self-analysis, others, on the basis of it, decide to change their whole lifestyles.

They may, for example, have been pressurized by their parents to follow some formally structured career while they themselves would rather have done something quite different, such as write poetry or paint pictures. At this point in their lives, having taken time to find out more about themselves, and their thoughts and feelings, they may decide to be true to themselves and their personal aspirations and turn their backs on their careers to do something that will bring them more fulfilment.

Some decide not only to leave the work they have been doing but the whole environment in which they have been living. Reflection on their lives has brought them a realization of the futility of their existence and a dislike of the materialism that has brought so much stress into their lives. They feel a need not only to get back to themselves but to get back to nature and a simpler way of life.

It is in such circumstances that, for example, a London stockbroker, used to a highly paid job and an affluent city lifestyle, might abandon his way of life and buy a croft in some remote part of Scotland with a view to living off the land and leading a virtually self-sufficient life. Of course, such dramatic changes do not always work out, and sometimes the stockbroker, or his equivalent, discovers that the whole thing was a wild romantic dream and hastily sells up the croft to return to the affluence of Surrey. Still, at least he will have learnt something about his true self, even although it might have proved an expensive venture.

New Age travelling

The desire to lead a simple, non-materialistic life does not necessarily involve rather a solitary life. The later decades of the twentieth century have seen the evolvement of the New Age travellers. These are people who seek to find a less materialistic, simpler, more golden age, but they wish to do so in the company of others who share their philosophy. There are often various other aspects to their philosophy, such as a concern for the environment and animal rights, a preference for natural remedies rather than formal medicine, and a leaning towards more ancient religions. New Age travellers are also intent on finding themselves, but they choose to do so in a communal, peripatetic way, moving on in vans and caravans from place to place and in doing so frequently falling foul of landowners or the police. Their desire to shake off the shackles of materialism and to lead a freer, less restricted life has something in common with the Hippies of the 1960s.

Retreats

Of course, not everyone who feels the need to take time

out to reflect on who he or she is, and how he or she feels, changes an entire lifestyle, whether to go off alone or as part of a group. As we have seen, many people simply want to be alone for a while to sort themselves out. This can be done in quite a structured, formal way as well as in the informal way described above. One example of this more formal way of taking time for reflection and self-exploration is the retreat, a place, as the name suggests, where one can get away from it all.

Retreats vary quite a bit. Some are extremely Spartan, encouraging one to concentrate on the mind, soul and spirit, rather than on the needs and delights of the body. Others are less basic, providing at least a minimum standard of comfort, although one should obviously not expect pampered luxury from a retreat. Some retreats are more organized and structured than others and provide lectures, discussions and workshops on various subjects for those who wish to attend. Others leave people more to their own devices, leaving them to meditate or pray and reflect as they wish.

Many retreats are religious in nature. Some of these relate to one of the Christian denominations, and people attend them to spend time in prayer and Bible study as well as to spend time in reflection. Other retreats of a religious nature relate to one of the eastern religious movements rather than to Christianity. In such retreats people tend to spend a good deal of time in meditation.

Yet other retreats of a religious nature may be based on the teachings on one of the sects that have become popu-

lar in the later decades of the twentieth century. Retreats
may differ widely in their nature, but they have one important thing in common—they provide the opportunity
for people to get out of the world for a while, to have time
for self-exploration and perhaps to achieve a degree of
spiritual and mental refreshment.

For some people a short time spent at a retreat proves not
to be enough. They feel the need to get out of the world
for a longer time in order to spend time communing with
themselves, and often with God. Such people sometimes
choose to join religious communities for a time in order to
find themselves and come to terms with themselves.

Personal growth and women's groups

Several people feel that, although they are not in need of
someone, such as a psychotherapist, to direct their journey
to their inner selves, they might be more inclined to initi-
ate such a journey and to persist with it if they had some
support. Some such people look for some sort of group to
join. In particular the later years of the twentieth century
has seen the rise of a number of what are known as personal growth societies, which are in many ways a later
form of the consciousness-raising groups popular in the
1970s.

Such societies often attract people who feel that they
have not achieved what they feel they should have
achieved in life. They feel stunted in some way or feel that
they have taken a wrong direction somewhere along the
path of their lives. The members of such societies, in their

efforts to achieve their aims, often begin with an attempt
to get to know their true selves and to find out how they
have become what they are. Until they do so they feel that
they cannot come to terms with themselves or maximize
their potential by finding out their true capabilities.

There are groups, other than personal growth societies,
that people join in order to find out more about themselves. We have seen in the previous chapter that many
people join self-help groups, but these tend to be people
who have a particular problem for which they seek the
help of group-members. Other people, for example, might
join a women's group.

Such groups became very popular in the later decades of
the twentieth century with the rise of feminism and the interest in the Women's Movement. The initial aim of a
women's group is not specifically to allow the members to
explore their inner selves. Many are formed with the aim
of discussing issues that are important to women and are
many and varied. They include such issues as equal opportunities in the workplace, equal pay, health issues,
such as screening for breast cancer, childcare, domestic
violence—several such groups were often formed initially
simply to discuss women's literature.

Although women's groups were not necessarily started
with the intention of leading their members to explore
their inner consciousness, they often have this effect.
When women begin to discuss the role of women in society and how it has changed in recent years, it often leads
them to begin to think about their own individual roles in

society and within the family, and to reassess themselves, their achievements and aspirations. They have, in fact, begun a journey to find their inner selves, although the original journey was designed to explore the standing and potential of women in the world.

For hundreds of years women were totally underestimated, and the struggle to assert themselves and to establish even a relatively fair position for themselves in society has been an extremely hard one. The fact that they had to put up a joint fight in order to achieve this, however, brought them together in a spirit of sisterhood and raised their consciousness of what it means to be a woman and the problems that this can bring. This encouraged the habit of joint discussion over women's issues.

Men, on the other hand, who for hundreds of years were unquestioningly acknowledged to be the superior sex, never had to group together to achieve their rights. Thus they have never really felt the necessity, or had the opportunity, to consider as a group what it means to be a man and the problems that this can bring. They therefore never really acquired the habit of joint male discussion about issues that are specifically male. Because of this, it has taken much longer for men to form self-help groups solely for them, and so this has not been a usual way for men to embark on an attempt to find their inner selves. Of course, for many years there have been men's clubs, but these were social rather than discussion groups, and certainly few would raise such subjects as men's health within the walls of a men's club.

In the closing years of the twentieth century things are beginning to change with respect to men's group. More men are beginning to feel the need to meet to discuss joint issues with other men and to receive support. These issues are often very specific ones. For example, men who are single parents sometimes form groups, or men who are separated or divorced and feel the need to fight for their rights as fathers sometimes do likewise. In addition, men are beginning to become aware of health problems that are specific to the male sex, and it is extremely feasible that this concern may give rise to the formation of more specifically male groups.

Another reason why men are beginning to group together in a way that has been common in women for some time relates to their concern for their rights and for their standing in society, the very issues that first drew women together. Because of women's success in the workplace, and because of the lack of employment opportunities generally, men have begun to feel threatened and to think that the assertion of women's rights has gone too far at the expense of their own.

It is highly likely that such feelings will lead to men getting together to discuss the situation and what can be done about it. If the formation of purely male groups continues to increase, it will certainly encourage individual men to explore their inner selves simply because such groups will set them thinking about their individual lives and roles in the same way that they set women thinking about theirs.

Thus, some people find the way to self-exploration

through membership of some kind of discussion group, whether or not they had that specific intention when they became members. Others feel that self-exploration is a more solitary pursuit. We have seen above how some people set out to achieve this, such as by going off by themselves or by going to a religious retreat.

Relaxation

Another and increasingly common method of getting in touch with one's inner self using one's own resources is through meditation. Mention has been made in the preceding chapter of how an interest in eastern religions and spiritual movements arose in the West in the 1960s. This in turn inspired an interest in meditation, which is often an essential part of such religions, even among people who do not embrace the whole religion.

An essential part of meditation is relaxation. Some people begin with relaxation and move on to meditation. Others find that relaxation alone fulfils their needs. They find that through relaxation they can unwind totally and free themselves from a buildup of stress. By devoting time and space to completely relaxing themselves and to making their minds completely free of the accumulation of thoughts and worries that usually occupy our twentieth-century minds, they feel that through relaxation alone they can commune with themselves and so explore their inner selves. In screening out the world, they give themselves the chance of looking into their subconscious, in the way that other people achieve through meditation.

Of course, there are degrees of relaxation, and some people use relaxation techniques simply to de-stress themselves. It represents a therapeutic pause in an overcrowded life. Others, again, see it as an opportunity to make time for themselves, to clear the mind of all the impedimenta that has built up there, and to unleash emotions and memories. For this second group, relaxation is a stage on a journey of exploration, even a final stage.

Relaxation techniques vary with the preference of the individual, and it is important for everyone who is interested in relaxation to find the method that is right for him or her. Some people, even if they lead highly stressed lives, find it easy to relax. Others find it extremely difficult, often thinking that they have no time for such a pursuit and often imagining that they will find it boring since they assume, quite wrongly, that deep relaxation is essentially a zombie-like state in which your level of consciousness is markedly dimmed.

Generally, people, especially those who are just beginning to learn relaxation techniques, like to find a comfortable position, although not a position that induces sleep, in order to be able to relax. Such a position varies from person to person. For example, some like to lie on the floor and others prefer to lean back in a comfortable chair. As long as you are comfortable, but not too comfortable, it really does not matter. People who have mastered the art of relaxation after much practice can go into their relaxation routine anywhere, but there is no point in putting obstacles in your way to begin with.

Comfort should also be considered when choosing clothes for relaxation sessions. Loose and comfortable clothing is considerably more conducive to relaxation than the rather tight suit that you may have worn to the office. If you are trying to slough off the worries of the day, you are less likely to achieve your aim if you are constantly aware of the tightness of your waistband.

It is important deliberately to set aside some time each day for your relaxation session. We all know how easy it is to have good intentions but somehow never find the time to carry these out. A little self-discipline is necessary to make some time for oneself, and it is easier to do this on a regular basis, rather than simply snatch a few minutes at a different time each day, at least until your relaxation session becomes a central part of your life. Again, people who are experienced in relaxation techniques can snatch a few minutes anywhere to go into their routine and de-stress themselves, but it takes some considerable time to achieve such expertise.

If you are just embarking on a relaxation programme, it is also important to provide yourself with somewhere quiet and private to set about the process. Until you have learnt something about the art of switching off, it is not fair to yourself to try out your relaxation technique in busy or noisy surroundings. It is all too easy to become distracted and then to assume that you are not a suitable candidate for relaxation. In time you may become one of those lucky people who can go into a relaxation programme anywhere, no matter how noisy or stressful your surroundings are, but it is rather foolish to assume that you will be able to do this right away.

Physical considerations must be thought of if you are contemplating a relaxation programme. Not only does clothing, place and time have to be considered but also the state of one's stomach. If you have just eaten a very heavy meal and go into your relaxation technique, you are very likely to fall asleep. On the other hand, if you have not eaten all day and are absolutely ravenous, you will very likely find it difficult to take your mind off your hunger long enough to concentrate on your relaxation technique.

Time, space, clothing and the state of the stomach are important to the person embarking on a relaxation programme, but there are other things that will help would-be relaxers to achieve their aim. One of these is a concentration on breathing techniques. Most of us, although we are probably unaware of the fact, have a shallow, erratic breathing pattern, in keeping with our busy, erratic lives. Controlled, regular breathing, however, is important both in relaxation and meditation. Apart from anything else, it induces a sense of calm that is central to both of these.

In order to master the breathing techniques used in relaxation and meditation programmes, it is worth becoming aware of the timing of the four-second breath, which is the basis of many breathing techniques. You breathe in to a count of four and breathe out to a count of four, often holding the breath at the top of the lungs to a count of two in between breathing in and breathing out, and holding the lungs empty to the count of two in between breathing out and breathing in again. If you practise this a few times by the clock, you will learn to judge the timing without recourse to a clock or watch and will be able to perform automatically the breathing techniques based on the four-second sequence.

Concentration on breathing directs one's thoughts away from the day's concerns and problems and enables one to concentrate purely on oneself. Perhaps the best-known example of using breathing techniques to induce relaxation and to divert concentration from problems, or in this particular case pain, is its use in natural childbirth. Expectant mothers are taught a series of regular breathing techniques at antenatal classes so that they might put these into practice during labour and so decrease their pain levels and the levels of drugs that are otherwise necessary.

Breathing techniques are thus an important part of thought-control or concentration-direction. Another effective way to accomplish this is by muscular relaxation techniques. This involves concentration on parts of the body in turn, for example, on the legs, and on how to recognize tension and relaxation in the muscles related to these. Total relaxation occurs when you are able to concentrate on the whole body part by part, getting each part to relax. More information on relaxation of body parts is given further on in the chapter in the discussion on meditation. As with concentration on breathing, concentration on relaxed muscles or parts of the body helps to direct one's concentration away from the problems and pressures of one's life.

Obviously, there is more to advanced relaxation and meditation techniques than can be described here. For anyone interested in the subject, however, there is a great deal of help available. There are various books on the subject obtainable either from your public libraries—although these are so popular now that you may have to reserve them—or from bookshops. Also there are various classes and courses run throughout the country so that people can acquire the essential techniques of relaxation that they can then practise by themselves.

Whether or not you join a class is a matter of personal preference. Some people find that it helps them to get started on something if they make the commitment to join a class. Others find it more difficult to follow written instructions given in a book than spoken instructions given by a teacher or class leader. Both such groups will obviously opt for a class, but many others are quite happy to follow written instructions at home at their own pace, perhaps seeking the advice of a friend with some knowledge of the subject.

Some people who opt for the home-based situation find that relaxation tapes are extremely helpful. These are readily available, and many of them talk would-be relaxers through relaxation techniques or a whole relaxation programme. A degree of self-discipline and concentration is required to get started on such a tape scheme, it being all to easy to buy the tape and put it in a drawer or to use it for a few minutes, get diverted and decide that it is not for you. People who persist with them, however, tend to swear by them, at least in the early stages of their relaxation programmes, when they are in need of a kickstart routine. Others claim that they find them annoying and even patronizing. As with most things in life, the tapes tend to vary in quality.

There are also people, particularly people who see relaxation simply as a way to unwind after a hard day's work rather than as a means to get more in touch with themselves, who find some ordinary music tapes helpful in their relaxation programmes. Such tapes should not be too stimulating, or they will defeat the purpose, or too soporific, or they will send the would-be relaxer to sleep. Something reasonably quiet, fairly middle-of-the road and fairly repetitive is usually what is required, but, of course, choice of music is very much a matter of personal taste and preference.

Massage

Other people associate relaxation with massage. Although to some extent this can be self-administered, in that one can massage those areas of the body that one can reach with ease, such as the legs, arms and feet, it is one area in this chapter where a little outside help should be used to augment the self-help. Massage by a friend or family member, or by a professional, is more common and probably more relaxing. It is unfortunate that professional massage has become associated in some circles and in some areas of the country with prostitution, because some brothels are euphemistically known as massage parlours.

This should not discourage people from seeking professional massage, as there are many people working in the field who simply practise the art of massage without any sexual overtones.

Massage consists of the techniques of stroking, both deep and superficial, kneading and skin rolling, the latter being performed on loose areas of the skin, such as can occur on the upper arms and abdomen. If done on a head-to-toe basis, massage can take some considerable time, and so the person undertaking it should be prepared for this. Agitating about time will simply undo the good done by the massage.

If performed by professionals, massage is not a technique for the unduly modest. It achieves best results if the person receiving the massage is either naked or else dressed in the scantiest of underwear. Also, it should be carried out on a firm surface, such as a table, a firm couch or the floor in a room that is comfortably warm. People will find it difficult to relax if they are cold, and the person performing the massage will be faced with a mass of goose pimples.

Aromatherapy

Some people performing—or receiving—massage prefer to use some form of lubricant, although this is not an essential part of massage. In the later years of the twentieth century massage with aromatherapy oils became extremely popular, and aromatherapy generally became much associated with relaxation and the getting rid of the effects of stress as well as with natural healing and alternative medicine.

Aromatherapy is a kind of holistic therapy that uses essential oils and aims not only to achieve relaxation and healing but also to achieve and maintain physical and mental equilibrium. The use of aromatic oils in healing is an ancient one. They were used in ancient Egypt almost three thousand years before Christ for medicinal as well as for cosmetic purposes and for embalming their dead. The Greeks also made use of plants and herbs in medicine, as did the Arab physicians later. Knights who had taken part in the Crusades brought back from the East to Europe perfumes and the knowledge of how to distil them. The Europeans did not have many of the aromatic, gum-yielding trees that were common in the East, but they used the aromatic shrubs that were native to the Mediterranean, such as lavender, rosemary and thyme, together with other herbs and plants.

Many forms of plant medicine were used in Europe throughout the Middle Ages and during the Tudor era. By the seventeenth century, however, chemical compounds were beginning to replace the use of plants in medicine, although many of the active ingredients of medicinal plants, such as quinine, morphine and atropine, found a place in the new medicine. The plant-based substances, especially in the twentieth century, began to be replaced by synthetic drugs.

Then, in the later decades of the twentieth century, there came a movement towards natural things generally and a movement towards natural things in medicine in particular. There was a reaction against formal medicine, and various forms of alternative medicine began to be popular. These included acupuncture, homoeopathy, herbal medicine, hypnosis, and so on, and particular attention was placed on holistic medicine, to treating the body and the mind as a whole.

As part of this movement towards natural, non-drug-based forms of medicine, aromatherapy has become very popular, and the essential oils have become generally available, although these tend to vary in quality. In fact, the modern aromatherapy movement began in France in the early part of the twentieth century when René Maurice Gattefosse, a chemist in his family's perfume company, developed an interest in the medicinal aspect of the oils used in perfumery. His discovery that lavender was a good antiseptic and an aid to healing when he burnt his hand and plunged it into neat oil of lavender increased his interest further. He coined the word 'aromatherapie' in a scientific paper and published a book of this title in 1928.

It took much longer for aromatherapy to become popular in Britain, but it began to become extremely popular in the 1980s, the decade when people began to appreciate the full effects of stress. Gradually, however, it caught on, and several books began to be published on the subject. A great many people have set themselves up as aromatherapy specialists, providing aromatherapy-based massage and giving advice on the use of essential oils. As with many so-called specialists in the alternative medicine fields, it is important to find someone who has some bona fide expertise in the field of aromatherapy. It is easy to acquire some kind of minimal qualification and create the impression that one has far more knowledge and experience than one actually has. In view of this, it is important to seek advice, and preferably a personal recommendation, before going for a consultation with an aromatherapist.

One might be forgiven for thinking that one could not go far wrong with the use of essential oils. This is quite wrong, however. Essential oils are in fact very potent and can have a powerful effect on the body or mind, or on conditions of the mind or body, and there are some conditions in which certain oils should not be used. For example, certain essential oils, such as rosemary, juniper, basil and clary sage, should be avoided in pregnancy, particularly in the early stages of it. It is extremely important, therefore, to obtain good advice, either from a knowledgeable person or a reliable book.

People use aromatherapy for various purposes. Some use it to help with a medical condition, such as lavender to try to help reduce high blood pressure, jasmine for depression, sandalwood for infections of the urinary tract, fennel for flatulence or digestive disorders, ginger for nausea or travel sickness, cypress for menstrual problems, tea-tree as an antiseptic for infected areas, juniper to help reduce fluid retention, black pepper for muscular pain or fatigue, and so on. There is a wide range of essential oils, and many of them are recommended for several conditions.

For example, lavender is an analgesic, an antiseptic and an anti-inflammatory agent as well as being useful in some skin conditions, insomnia, depression, high blood pressure, and a number of other disorders.

Not everyone uses aromatherapy to cure or relieve medical disorders. Others use it because it gives them a sense of wellbeing, and many use it for purposes of relaxation. We have seen above how many people opt for massage as a means to relaxation. It is now common for people to combine massage and aromatherapy to help them relax by having a massage with essential oils either from a friend or family member or from a professional masseur or masseuse. When combined with base oils to dilute them, the essential oils are very readily absorbed through the skin, and so they make the ideal massage oil. The person applying the massage will choose a blend of oils to suit the particular client, and a great deal of skill is required to get this right. Essential oils should not be used neat.

People who regularly have massage sessions with a blend of oils especially designed to relax them often indicate that they are left after the massage sessions with a great sense of calm and peace, which is an excellent frame of mind for exploring one's deeper self. The essential oils, however, need not be used just as a massage lubricant to achieve relaxation. Many people use a few drops of essential oils in a bath to rid themselves of stress and become more relaxed. Others prefer to use them as an inhalation. In both these cases, as with massage, it is important to find out about the properties and uses of the various essential oils because by no means all of them make you feel relaxed, some having the effect of stimulating you.

As has been indicated above, the extent to which relaxation helps people to explore their inner selves depends to a great extent on the degree of relaxation achieved. The deeper the degree of relaxation the more likely it is that you will be able to get more in touch with yourself.

Yoga

Many people either add a yoga component to their relaxation programme or take up yoga as a regular pursuit to increase the degree of their relaxation. There are several forms of yoga, the word being a general term for various spiritual disciplines followed by devotees of Hinduism to attain a higher consciousness, and also being the name of one of the six orthodox systems of Indian philosophy. It is an integral part of Hinduism, and its name derives from the 'yoke' that binds the individual self and universal self together. A common form practised in the West is Hatha Yoga, which emphasizes physical control and postures.

Yoga, as we know it, is now very popular in this country. It is based on a system of physical exercises and postures and of controlled breathing. You will find many classes on yoga throughout the country, but many of them are based on a rather watered-down form of the original concept, there being often not much concentration on the spiritual aspect of yoga. Of course, this is by no means always the case, and you may well be fortunate enough to find a teacher who will bring this extra dimension to the class.

Whether or not you are looking for a teacher who will be able to impart the Hindu principles of yoga, or whether you are simply looking to it as a potential aid to relaxation or to de-stressing yourself, you should spend some time taking advice so that you may find someone competent. As with other areas of alternative therapy and medicine, where there are few hard and fast qualifications required, not everyone who has set up as a yoga teacher is truly competent. It is important to be taught by someone with training and experience, if only so that you may adopt the relevant postures without in any way injuring yourself. Yoga is certainly one method of relaxation that needs to be taught, although after you have mastered the basic techniques you can practise them alone at home

Even if the spiritual content is either missing or not very strongly emphasized, yoga is for many people an excellent way of achieving relaxation and a sense of wellbeing and peace. Partly because of the degree of concentration involved, many people also find yoga a good way of blocking out the world, bringing them calm and inner peace and giving them the opportunity and means of exploring their inner selves.

Meditation

Meditation is yet another way in which people set out to rid themselves of stress and perhaps embark on a journey of self-discovery. As we have seen above, relaxation is one of the components of this, and many people who successfully establish a relaxation programme for themselves go no further, seeing relaxation as an end in itself. Others, however, go on to master, or to try to master, the art of meditation. Although meditation is the cornerstone of many religions and cults, and in many cases corresponds to prayer, people who decide to practise meditation do not necessarily adopt the other aspects of the religion or cult.

The verb 'to meditate' can mean simply to think deeply about something, but meditation in the form that we are currently considering it is more than just deep thought. Like thought, meditation is a mental discipline, but it requires even more concentration than our usual thought processes. It is indeed a state of mind in which all thoughts are concentrated on a single point or subject. Such concentration is very difficult to achieve and takes time, patience and persistence. Our minds have a tendency to wander from subject to subject, and concentration on one point has to be worked at.

Many people give up on meditation at an early stage since they lack the patience and commitment to come anywhere near achieving the degree of concentration that is necessary to reap its benefits. People who do persist with the practice of meditation, however, often say that the benefits that meditation has brought to them have been very great indeed, one of the most important being that it has brought them inner peace and inner knowledge, which has in turn brought self-realization, central to any journey of self-discovery.

Some people say that they meditate to bring the mind into a state of calmness and concentration so that it can explore its consciousness. Others view it as a way of achieving a greater clarity of perception, or of finding a new way of perceiving the world and of relating to it. Others again feel that through it they can come into contact with their very soul or even with God. This sounds extremely interesting, but how do you set about meditating? As has already been pointed out, the physical conditions that are conducive to deep relaxation tend also to be conducive to meditation.

You should be comfortable, but not so comfortable as to be in danger of falling asleep, since the aim of meditation is to stay alert but relaxed. Some people meditate successfully lying on the floor but others find that it is difficult not to feel sleepy in this position. Others try to adopt the lotus position, as Buddhist monks do, but sitting cross-legged for any length of time is extremely uncomfortable for most of us. Basically, you should experiment until you find the posture that is right for you. Many people find that sitting upright with their backs against something, such as sitting on a reasonably firm chair, is the posture most conducive to successful meditation. Comfortable, loose clothes are also important, as is the fact that the room chosen for meditation should be at a comfortable temperature.

As is the case with relaxation, it is important to find somewhere quiet when you are teaching yourself to meditate. After you have gained some mastery in the art you may be able to meditate in noisy surroundings, although many people retain a preference for a calm environment away from the hurly-burly of life, but at first you need as few distractions as possible if you are to achieve the required level of concentration.

It is, of course, important to make time for meditation in our lives, if we are going to take it in any way seriously. Haphazardly trying to fit it in at odd intervals is obviously not going to work, and some rearrangement of one's lifestyle may be necessary even in order to set aside fifteen minutes or half-an-hour regularly in a crowded day. Naturally, choosing the same period each day helps, as this becomes part of a regular routine and we are less likely to give it up. A great many people choose to get up earlier than they did formerly and devote this extra time at the start of the day to meditation, when they are feeling refreshed after a night's sleep. Others prefer to set aside time in the evening, either because they cannot face the thought of getting up earlier or because they feel that meditating in the evening is an excellent way of losing the stress that has built up during the day.

Breathing is as important in meditation as it is in relaxation and in several of the eastern religions and philosophies. A pattern of breathing that is controlled and rhythmic, of the kind described under the discussion on relaxation, will induce the feeling of calm that is necessary for concentration. If our breathing is erratic, it is often a sign that our thoughts and emotions are disturbed, and so if we learn to make it measured and controlled we can learn to impose some regularity and calm on our minds.

The next stage in meditation is also like one already re-

ferred to under relaxation above. It is relaxation of the
parts of the body and the muscles. This is done by directing your thoughts to each part of your body in turn and
flexing and relaxing the muscles in it until the body part is
totally relaxed. You should not try to hurry this part of the
exercise of meditation as it requires time and patience,
particularly in the early stages before you have gained any
expertise. Some people find that it helps actually to address each part of the body in turn, whether silently or
aloud, as 'My neck is relaxing' or 'Relax, neck!' Others
feel that they can more easily induce a state of relaxation
in each body part by imagining that it feels heavy.

When a comfortable posture has been found, a controlled pattern of breathing established, and the whole body is
relaxed and calm, it is time to begin concentrating on a
particular subject. Some spiritual traditions favour particular subjects. For example, in Buddhism the focus is
often on human qualities or conditions, such as kindness,
compassion, happiness or joy as subjects for meditation,
while in Christianity the focus might be on some aspect of
Christ's life or his teachings or beliefs.

Symbols and their exploration are also popular objects
of focus. For example, one might select the circle and reflect on its associations with endlessness or completeness,
or one might select a symbol with religious associations,
such as the cross of Christianity, the star of David of the
Jewish faith, and so on.

The choice of subjects is virtually endless, however, and,
especially when you have acquired some expertise in

meditation, the choice is yours. You may, for example, wish to focus on flowing water, an opening flower or a path through the woods. It is as well to start with something relatively simple, such as a particular primary colour or fire. It is not so much what one chooses to concentrate on that is important but one's success in concentrating.

Sometimes the focus of meditation is a word or short phrase that is repeated over and over again. It is sounded aloud in such a way that it vibrates and is called a mantra. Mantras are found in Hinduism and in Buddhism and have become common in Western meditation. Religious and spiritual traditions often use a mantra that evokes the name of God, but you can select any phrase that you like for your own personal mantra. You might, for example, experiment with using your own name. Especially in transcendental meditation, founded by Maharishi Mahesh Yogi, it is common for people to ask their gurus to supply a personal mantra for them.

Reciting a mantra has its equivalents in other forms of religion. For example, people chant or intone prayers in church. In the Catholic church people sometimes murmur over their rosaries. Some people claim that the actual content of the mantra is important; others claim that the content is utterly unimportant and you can use a nonsense word or phrase if you like. Basically, your goal in reciting a mantra is to concentrate completely on chanting and to become unaware of anything else.

It is often difficult to concentrate on a specific point or

subject and to clear one's mind of everything else. People who are having difficulty in emptying their minds in a meditational session sometimes find that their concentration is helped if they direct their attention to something small, such as a button or a flower, or if they direct it towards the random lights that appear behind the eyelids, particularly if the eyes are opened and closed a few times.

We have seen how much meditation uses something to focus on. In Zen Buddhism, however, the basic daily meditation practice is called 'zazen', meaning 'just sitting'. In this there is no chosen subject to focus on. You just focus on the mind itself. The object is to achieve a state in which you can watch your mind working but not become involved in its contents. This detachment creates space in your mind.

Indeed, one of the purposes of meditation generally is to make space in our minds, leaving room for higher thoughts and for communication with one's inner or higher self. If the desire to know yourself has been one of the reasons why you have taken up meditation, then you can use this as the focus of your meditation, starting with a phrase such as 'Know yourself' and the meaning and implications of that. You can then move on to focus on different aspects of your being, using your memories of the different stages of your life, the different emotional states you have known, and so on. You might even consider using the phrase 'Who am I?' as a starting point for one of your meditation sessions, hoping that in the course of the meditation you will find your true self.

This kind of meditation, performed in a structured way, has been called 'self-inquiry' by Ramana Maharishi. If this form of meditation is carried out on a strictly structured question-and-answer basis it is said to be very difficult to achieve and to require several months of practise in other structured forms of meditation.

There are people who are cynical about meditation, and most of us are very ill-informed about it. It is quite common, for example, to think of people who are meditating as rather weird people who go into self-imposed hypnotic trances. People who have been successfully meditating for some time, however, often speak of the inner knowledge that meditation has brought to them, and so, clearly, someone interested in exploring the inner self should try to master the techniques of it.

There are various ways in which people can learn the art of meditation. Since meditation by its very nature can easily be seen as a solitary pursuit, many people prefer to practise the art of meditation alone at home rather than in a group or in a class. Many of them may attend a class or seek out a teacher to learn the basic techniques and then choose to go it alone. Others feel that they would prefer to start from the beginning using their own devices and try to learn the basics from books or from friends who are also interested in meditation.

Some of those who take up meditation have a guru, or teacher, to teach them the basic techniques and philosophy and to provide future guidance when necessary. This is particularly true of those who take up transcendental meditation, frequently known as TM. In this from of meditation the guru often provides a personal mantra for the person undertaking meditation.

There are specialists in meditation who claim that serious, successful meditation cannot be undertaken without a teacher, but there are others who claim that this is not necessarily the case and that, furthermore, no teacher is better than a teacher who is not experienced and skilled enough in the art of meditation. Sadly, as with the various other routes to self-discovery that we have explored, there are people who lack sufficient experience and skill but who acquire enough of the superficial knowledge and of the jargon to set up as a teacher or guide.

What must be remembered is that meditation is a rigorous discipline of the mind, which requires practice, time and steady, regular hard work. Anyone seriously thinking of taking up meditation should be prepared for this and should be prepared for setbacks. It is not an easy path to sudden enlightenment.

These then are some of the ways by which people might help themselves towards a greater understanding of themselves. Some of these ways may depend, at least initially, on the help and guidance of others, but the onus is on the person seeking this understanding to make the time and effort—often considerable—to enable this to come about. Many have found that the effort and time involved were a small price to pay for the self-knowledge that they were able to uncover.

Chapter 4

Help from Beyond

There are people who, when they feel the need to get more in touch with themselves or to find out more about themselves, look to the paranormal for help. Some of the areas that we have already discussed in previous chapters are subject to a great deal of scepticism but none more so than the paranormal. People may scoff at the claims made on behalf of psychoanalysis or meditation but nothing like so heartily as they scoff at claims made on behalf of psychics, clairvoyants, fortune-tellers or astrologers. Yet there are those who derive much comfort from the activities of people who claim to be working in the field of the paranormal and who feel that the information and help that they have obtained from them has been instrumental in giving them a fuller, more accurate picture of themselves.

Just as commitment and self-discipline are necessary requirements for people who wish to get the most out of meditation, so belief is necessary for those who wish to get the most out of the paranormal. Many of us will have heard tales of an utter sceptic who went along with a friend who was intent on consulting a medium or a clairvoyant and was so impressed by the information given that instant conversion was the result. Nevertheless, people attempting to harness the paranormal in the course of their work prefer people who consult them to be firm believers if they are to achieve success with them.

There are, of course, many of us who have a slight interest in some aspects of the paranormal, although not a firm belief. For example, many of us turn automatically to the page in a newspaper or magazine that has 'the stars', as astrological predictions are informally known, but few of us are going to change our projected course of action for the day, or for our lives, on the basis of this. For most of us it is a bit of fun, although a very popular one, since a great many publications do carry some form of astrological prediction.

Spiritualism

Several people who become actively interested in the paranormal do so out of grief or distress. A relative of someone who has died may feel a desperate need to get in touch with the spirit of the deceased for some reason. Perhaps the person concerned had a quarrel with the relative, which was not resolved before death; perhaps the deceased was the only one who was in possession of a piece of information that is central to the person's life and wellbeing, and has taken the information to the grave. Perhaps the person concerned just needs to know that the spirit of the deceased relative is at peace.

People wishing or longing to make contact with the spirits of the dead usually consult a medium or spiritualist, who may organize a seance. Several people who have undertaken such a consultation have come away feeling convinced that contact has been made with the spirit of the deceased person and feeling a great sense of inner peace that they have sorted out with the dead person whatever was bothering them—even if, in fact, they have only put their own interpretation on something that has been said. They may have been experiencing inner turmoil for years, perhaps over an unsettled family feud, and may only now be capable of a state of calm that is conducive to exploring their inner selves.

The work of mediums is an area about which many people are sceptical. Certainly, it is true that the medium can elicit much information from the client seeking contact with the dead from a few searching questions. If the medium is experienced in this art of fishing for information, he or she—in fact many of them are women—will be able to glean a great deal of information without the client being aware of this. The client may then be absolutely amazed at the supposed paranormal powers of the medium in knowing all this and be inclined to believe anything that is said from then on.

In addition, people who have set themselves up as mediums and have had a great deal of practice with clients learn how to deduce a lot of information from the appearance, age, sex, speech, clothes, etc, of the client, in the way that a detective might do. They also become skilled

in the art of educated guesswork, which is an excellent aid
in their summing-up of the client, and clients may again
be amazed at what they assume to be knowledge gained
by paranormal means.

It is not the purpose of this book to defend or condemn
the work of mediums. Suffice it to say that if people derive comfort and inner peace from consulting them, then
who are we to deny them this comfort if no actual harm is
done? Problems can arise, however, and people should be
careful whom they consult.

Obviously, they should avoid paying out large sums of
money and should be wary of falling too much under the
power and influence of the medium—perhaps this advice
should best be directed at relatives, living ones obviously,
since people consulting mediums are sometimes in too
great a state of distress to be entirely rational. Many mediums, however, are simply local amateurs who perform the
service as a hobby or for a small fee. Often they conduct
regular seances, where several people gather round a table
and try to make contact with spirits of the dead.

Clairvoyance

Clairvoyants are another group of people whom some clients may consult in a state of distress, although others
may just go out of interest because a friend has gone and
been intrigued. The word 'clairvoyance' means the detection or acquiring of information, by some perception other
than that which we would regard as normal, that is, by
some kind of extrasensory perception.

People's reasons for consulting clairvoyants are many and various. Someone who is adopted and who is desperately seeking to know the whereabouts of a birth parent, having failed to do so by any of the more orthodox means described in the next chapter, might think of consulting a clairvoyant. Likewise, a parent whose son or daughter who has left home after a quarrel might seek a clairvoyant's advice on where to look for him or her. It is even not unknown for a clairvoyant to be consulted in the detection of crimes. For example, clairvoyant help might be sought in the location of the body of someone who is known to have been murdered but whose dead body has not been found.

Again, it is not the role of this book to pontificate on the case for and against clairvoyance. Several of the comments mentioned in the discussion on mediums could be applicable also to clairvoyants. For example, as in the case of mediums, clairvoyants by skilful questioning can sometimes obtain quite a lot of information from the clients themselves without the clients even being aware that they have given the information, and sometimes even without the clients realizing that they were in fact in possession of the said information.

Whether or not there is general scepticism about clairvoyants—although there tends to be slightly less scepticism about clairvoyants than there is about mediums—does not matter if the individual client derives some kind of peace or even hope from the consultation, as long as he or she does not part with any large sums of money and

does not come too much under the influence of the clairvoyant. A person seeking a birth parent may, for example,
be given enough hope, even if not accurate information, to
inspire him or her to go on with the search, which might
eventually prove successful. Likewise, the parent seeking
the whereabouts of a missing teenager might receive similar motivation and inspiration.

It is possible that people might seek a consultation with a
clairvoyant with the specific intention of using the experience to learn more about their inner selves. Even if this is
not their avowed intention, it is possible that something
they are told, or something that they think they have been
told, will bring them peace in some way, so that they are
less anxious and more likely to be able reflect on who they
really are. The information imparted, or thought to have
been imparted, may also alter the life of the person who
has consulted the clairvoyant in such a way as to make the
person reassess his or her life, aims and hopes, and so give
some thought to the inner self.

Fortune-telling

Some clairvoyants claim to be able to predict the future,
although, strictly speaking, this is more precognition—the
detection of information about future events by extrasensory perception—than clairvoyance. The role of the clairvoyant thus sometimes becomes confused with that of the
fortune-teller.

To many of us the word 'fortune-teller' conjures up pictures of a village resident dressed up as a gypsy pretend-

ing to tell people's fortunes in a tent or booth at the local fair, inviting people to cross her hand with silver as a donation to charity. Obviously, hardly anyone would dream of taking this kind of supposed forecasting of the future seriously, although if the person taking the role of fortune-teller has lived in the village for a long time then her predictions, based on her knowledge and observation of the people consulting her, might well be quite near the mark.

Thus, to many of us fortune-telling is a bit of a joke, although it is also very popular. It would take a bit of persuasion for many of us to go and consult a supposed teller of the future officially and professionally. Nevertheless, if a friend of the family happened to be someone who read the tea leaves as a hobby, a surprising number of us would find ourselves handing over our empty teacups to be read, even although we might scoff at the prediction of a journey overseas or a meeting with a dark stranger.

Sadly, a development of modern living has interfered rather drastically with the art of teacup reading. The days when people made tea with tea leaves taken from a packet declined with the later decades of the twentieth century. The modern use of tea bags means there is no deposit of tea leaves in the cup and so nothing to read.

Of course, packets of tea are still available, and there are still some people, mainly older women, who read tea leaves, sometimes as part of a wider fortune-telling repertoire, although it does carry more homely connotations than other forms—it sounds more impressive if you call it by its fancier name of tasseomancy. There are several other forms of fortune-telling, although not all fortune-tellers practise all of them.

Although many of us regard, or at least claim to regard, fortune-telling in a purely light-hearted way, there are also many people who take it seriously, or at least are half-inclined to take it seriously. They may not admit to it, given the degree of scepticism among their friends, but some people might well see consulting a fortune-teller as a step in a journey of self-discovery. A sly look into their likely future might change the whole way they look at themselves and cause them to stop and try to assess who they really are and where they are going. Even an arch nonbeliever might do this if a friend was engaged in a similar pursuit.

The classic image of the fortune-teller is of someone looking into a crystal ball, and divination by this means is known as crystallamonacy. Originally, rock crystal was used, although beryl serves the purpose better. Both of these are expensive, and crystal balls nowadays are most often made of clear glass, although even they are far from being cheap. The interpreter of the crystal ball is called a 'scryer'.

He or she—many fortune-tellers are women—often ask the person who has asked for a consultation to think of the problem or area of life with which he or she wishes guidance. Sometimes the person will be asked to put his or her hands close to the crystal ball—many scryers are reluctant to have their clients actually touch the crystal ball in case the supposed psychic energy level might be interfered with and the power of the crystal ball destroyed.

Scryers say that the crystal ball becomes cloudy at first, and as it clears, images appear that enable them to interpret the future. These images are often just cloudy masses of an indistinct shape, the colour of these being important. For example, white clouds suggest good fortune, black clouds suggest evil, green suggests hope, and red suggests danger or hatred. Some scryers claim to be able to see actual shapes and even whole scenes from the future.

Not all fortune-tellers use crystal balls. Many use cards. A great many use ordinary playing cards, efforts to predict the future by this means being called 'cartomancy'. Not only many professional fortune-tellers practise cartomancy but also a great deal of enthusiastic amateurs, who learn up the various meanings that have been given to individual cards, or to combinations of cards, by tradition. For example, the nine of spades is said to indicate bad luck, loss and conflict; the eight of diamonds a pleasant journey or a late marriage; the king of clubs a dark-haired, honest, kind man; the ten of hearts joy, love, good fortune and the realization of ambition.

Of course it is not as simple as this sounds. If you are going to take up card-reading seriously you will have to put in a great deal of time and effort. There are various skills involved, as well as a good memory, and some at least would claim that to be successful some psychic powers are also necessary.

To turn to more mundane matters, there are various

methods of laying the cards out, and the number of cards used varies from card-reader to card-reader. In addition, some card-readers claim a changed meaning for a reversed card, as is the case with tarot cards, while others do not.

Another method of fortune-telling that is becoming increasingly popular uses tarot cards. The standard tarot pack consists of 78 cards, instead of the 52 cards of the ordinary playing-card pack. The pack consists of trumps, or Major Arcana, numbered from 1 to 21, together with the fool, not numbered but often assigned zero, 0, and the Minor Arcana, or four suits.

The Major Arcana include the magician, the high priestess, the empress, the emperor, the hierophant (or high priest), the lovers, the chariot, justice, the hermit, the wheel of fortune, strength, the hanged man, death, temperance, the devil, the tower, the star, the moon, the sun, judgement, and the world. The four suits of the Minor Arcana are swords, wands (also sometimes known as rods, sceptres, staves or batons), cups, and pentacles (also sometimes known as coins or discs).

Although tarot-reading has become extremely popular recently, with a great many cards with different, modern designs available on the market, it is in many ways a more complicated procedure than fortune-telling with ordinary playing-cards, and there is held to be a spiritual aspect to tarot-reading. As is the case with crystal-ball reading, the person wishing to have the future predicted should ideally have a problem or issue in mind, and the person making

the reading, called the 'diviner', must be in the right frame
of mind and in surroundings that he or she finds conducive to concentration.

We have seen that traditionally various meanings are assigned to various cards in cartomancy, or fortune-telling
using playing cards. This is also true of the tarot cards. For
example, the nine of wands indicates strength to cope with
unexpected problems or readiness; the three of cups successful resolution, conclusions or healing; the eight of
swords crisis, conflict or difficulty in escaping; the six of
pentacles generosity or success shared with others.

In ordinary playing-card reading, some readers claim a
different meaning for a reversed card—reversed top to
bottom. In tarot it is a basic rule that reversed cards have a
different meaning. For example, the nine of wands,
which, as has been indicated above, means strength to
face unexpected problems, but when reversed it means
obstacles or adversity. Similarly, the six of pentacles
means generosity or success shared with others, but when
reversed it means greed, selfishness or envy.

Palmistry

Another common way of trying to predict the future is
palmistry, also sometimes known as cheiromancy. Palmistry sets out not only to predict the future but also to reveal things about the personality and life of the person
whose hand is being read, although reputable people engaged in palmistry are at pains to point out that one does
not actually predict the future by palmistry but, instead,

one indicates tendencies and, therefore, possibilities.

Many people become interested in palmistry as a hobby, thinking that it would be useful or fun to be able to read their own hands or those of their friends. A great many of these, however, give up the pursuit of palmistry very early on when they begin to realize just how complicated it is. In fact, to acquire any degree of skill in palmistry involves a great deal of time and effort to master the necessary knowledge and gain the necessary experience.

Palmistry involves studying the shape, size and general appearance of the hand, including the fingers and the length, thickness and positioning of the thumb. It also involves studying the slightly raised areas of the palm, known as mounts, such as Jupiter, Saturn, Mars, Venus, etc; the major lines on the palm—the heart line, which indicates emotional feeling, the head line, which indicates mental porches and intelligence, and the life line, which indicates physical wellbeing; the minor lines, which are not present on all hands and indicate processes such as the line of fate, the line of fortune (also known as the line of success), and the line of health. It is a complex area of study, not least because the lines on a palm are rarely as clearly etched and defined as they appear to be in illustrations in books on palmistry.

People who consult a competent palmist my well come away feeling that they have acquired a new insight into themselves and that they are now more in touch with themselves. People who consult palmists because of some particular problem, however, whether or not they reveal this to the palmist, may well be in a vulnerable state, as are the people who consult mediums and clairvoyants in grief or distress. Palmists must be extremely careful that they do not say anything that will cause further distress to someone in such a position.

Obviously, competent professional palmists are aware of this, and it is mostly enthusiastic amateurs who cause anxiety and distress in people, although they might not realize that they have done so. For example, they might have suggested, when commenting on lines in the palm, that the person whose hand it is may not live very long or may have a serious illness or injury at some point in the future.

In fact, this point is something that is relevant to everyone who is engaged in any form of fortune-telling, whether the fortune-teller is a professional or amateur. Again, the advice is directed at the enthusiastic amateur or the less competent, less experienced fortune-teller. It is particularly common for someone with a little knowledge of some form of fortune-telling, such as palmistry, card-reading or tea-leaf reading, to be having a light-hearted session with a friend and reveal something bad about the future, thinking that the friend is a total sceptic anyhow and will not for one minute believe it. Sceptic or not, it might well prey on the friend's mind.

Astrology
So far we have looked at mediums, clairvoyants, fortune-tellers and palmists, all of whom may be consulted by

people who are trying to find out something that will add in some way to the information that they have about themselves and that might well lead them to think more carefully about themselves and perhaps to reassess and replot their lives. Many people, however, who wish to know more about themselves do not turn to any of these but turn instead to an astrologer, or to astrology, since many people consult charts and books rather than an actual person.

As was mentioned early on in this chapter, astrology is very popular in this country, although many of us do not take it in any way seriously. Many people, however, take it very seriously indeed, and some astrologers report that in recent times they have not only seen an increase in the number of people consulting them but in the number of people who consult them specifically to use astrological means to get in touch with their inner selves. Just as there has been a move away from modern materialism, and a move towards New Age philosophy, alternative medicine and meditation, so there has been a move towards understanding the Zodiac.

Astrology is a much more complex subject than simply looking up one's horoscope in a magazine. According to astrology, the Zodiacal signs—Aries, Taurus, Gemini, Cancer, Leo, Virgo, Libra, Scorpio, Sagittarius, Capricorn, Aquarius and Pisces—confer certain characteristics on those who are born under them. Some people feel that by acquiring detailed information on these characteristics they can reach a deeper realization of themselves and their actions.

For some people this is enough, but others wish to delve even further into their astrological selves and consult an astrologer to get them to cast a personal birth chart. Some people even try to do this themselves, although it is a very complex business. You need to know the correct time of your birth, adjusted to Greenwich Mean time and taking account of any allowance for daylight-saving time. You also require an 'ephemeris', a book that gives the positions of the sun, the moon and planets at particular times. It also requires some skill at drawing or draughtsmanship since you are required to draw discs, although this skill is not so necessary these days when many people contemplating casting a birth chart might do so on their home computers.

Also important in astrology, particularly with reference to prediction, are the 'houses'. There are twelve of these, each one being connected with a specific area of life of the individual for whom the prediction is being made. For example, the first house is connected with self, the ego and appearance, and with beginnings, the fifth house is connected with leisure, pleasure, hobbies, children, creativity and light-hearted love affairs, and the tenth house with career, status and ambition, and so on.

As with palmistry, astrology is not so easy as it might appear at first sight. People who wish to study it in detail from books and who feel that by so doing they may get a clearer understanding of what makes them tick should be prepared to put much time and effort into the task. Many people consult a professional astrologer. They may wish, to acquire, for example, a birth chart, or an astrological prediction.

What has been said so far about astrology refers to Western astrology. There is now a growing interest in Chinese astrology, which has no connection with astrology as we are in the habit of thinking of it. It is based on twelve animal signs—the Rat, the Buffalo (or Ox), the Tiger, the Cat (or Rabbit or Hare), the Dragon, the Snake, the Horse, the Goat, the Monkey, the Rooster (or Cockerel), the Dog (or the Pig or Boar). The twelve animal year signs follow each other in a regular cycle. For example, 1989 was the year of the snake, as was 1977, 1965, and 1953, and so on.

It should be remembered that the Chinese astrological years do not correspond exactly to our calendar years, being based on the lunar year, and that the Chinese New Year begins on a different date each year. For example, 1989 began on 6 February, 1977 began on 28 February, 1965 on 21 February, 1953 on 14 February, and so on.

As with Western astrology, Chinese astrology is more complex than at first it might seem to be. The basis of the animal signs is that people born under the same animal sign, say that of the snake, will have some particular personality traits and characteristics in common, just as people born under the same sign of the Zodiac in Western astrology are thought to.

The animal signs, however, are not the whole story, because any prediction will also take into consideration the hour, day and month of the year of birth, as well as the actual year itself.

Dream interpretation

Thus if you feel that you wish to involve astrological influences in your journey of self-discovery, you have a choice at hand. If, however, you fancy neither astrology, nor any of the other fields mentioned in this chapter, as an aid to greater self-realization, or if indeed you have tried some or all of them but have found them wanting, you may find what you are looking for in dreams, or rather in the interpretation of them

A major problem of dream interpretation is that, although we all dream every night, we often do not remember doing so. Even if we do realize that we have been dreaming, and even if the dreams were quite vivid at the time, the details of the dream pass incredibly quickly, leaving us with no real memory of them. If you are interested in dream interpretation, it is helpful to keep paper and pen by the bed so that you can commit the dreams to paper as soon as possible before you forget them.

There is often much symbolism in dreams, and we should not try to interpret all dreams in a literal way. Nor should we assume that they are necessarily predictive, although there are many stories throughout history of instances where people are supposed to have received messages or warnings in dreams, whether or not they acted on them. Adolf Hitler, for example, leader of the Nazi movement in Germany, claimed that as a young corporal in a trench on the Somme during World War I he received a warning in a dream to leave the bunker where he was sleeping and that shortly after he did so the bunker was destroyed by a shell. Abraham Lincoln, the American president, was not so fortunate. He is said to have been warned in a dream of an assassination attempt, but he ignored the warning and was assassinated. Nevertheless, these are unusual cases, and there is no need to assume that someone is going to die just because you dream of his or her death.

If you are convinced that dream interpretation can help you find yourself, particularly if you have recurring dream motifs, you should consult someone with experience in this field. You should do the same if you seriously seek a prediction of the future based on your dreams—prediction on the basis of dreams is known as oneiromancy. If, however, you would just like to know more about the subject, you could invest in a book on the subject or borrow one from the local library.

Such books will tell you something about the interpretation of dreams and list various things and events that might be found in dreams, together with their suggested interpretation. For example, flying is said to be a sign of some kind of success in the near future or a sign of ambition. On the other hand, if you keep dreaming about flying and the flying always ends in you falling, this could indicate a sense of insecurity, a worry about failing or the possibility of a quarrel with someone.

It is, of course, important not to become too cast down or anxious if you think that you have come up with a particularly gloomy prediction. The whole subject is too complex and too open to speculation for you to have cause to worry. Various symbols can also have various interpretations.

These then are some of the ways in which the unknown can be involved in our attempts to find out more about ourselves or to find out what is likely to happen in the future. Many of these ways indicate either a revival or a renewed interest in ancient traditions, in keeping with our looking to the past for healing processes. Most of us would find something of interest in at least some of these, even if we are not wholly convinced by them. Others find some kind of comfort, and perhaps a new awareness of themselves, by seeking help from agencies that do not fall within the range of ordinary human experience.

Chapter 5

Genealogical Bewilderment—the Search for Birth Parents

Some of us feel that we cannot really know ourselves before we find out more about what made us what we are today. We feel that we need to know more about our early beginnings. In some cases the need to know about roots and family background is fairly historical to a greater or lesser degree.

Quite a lot might be known about parents, and possibly grandparents, but if the members of a family have been rather mobile over the decades and have moved from place to place it may be not be so easy to go beyond the grandparent stage. Finding out about ancestors and the various branches of the family can be a source of preoccupation for years, particularly if some family members have moved overseas.

To most of us, finding out more about our family tree is something in which we are vaguely interested, something that we might investigate when we have the time and leisure to do so, something that we somehow never seem to get round to. Others, however, for some reason feel a deep need to find out as much as possible about the early origins of their family, perhaps in the hope that this will help them towards a fuller realization of their own identity. They regard research into their roots as a vital part of their voyage of self-discovery.

This desire for historical information relating to family will be discussed in the next chapter, but there are people with a more pressing and immediate desire to know more about their family. These are the people who were adopted at birth or in their early years and who seek to find information not about historical ancestors but about their birth parents.

Someone who has not been adopted may well find it difficult to appreciate the agonizing need to find a real parent that is experienced by someone who has been adopted. It is by no means uncommon for people not to get on with their parents, either for all their lives or for certain phases of it. They thus, ostensibly at least, set no great store by parents, sometimes even joking rather tastelessly that they wished they were adopted so that they need feel no close relationship with the people who brought them up. To many who have been adopted, the need to find the people to whom they are genetically related can take over their whole lives. Without it they can feel a sense of rootlessness, almost a sense of non-identity. Indeed, this state has been called 'genealogical bewilderment', to emphasize the feelings of confusion that adopted people can experience.

The need to find at least one of the people who were physically responsible for one's birth has presumably always been there. Not so the opportunity. Legal adoption was introduced in England and Wales in 1926 and in Scotland in 1930, but it was not until 1975, when the law was changed to allow people access to their original birth certificates, that the likelihood of finding one's real or birth parents became a viable possibility—in Scotland people over the age of 17 have always had the right of access to their original birth certificates, but this was a fact not generally known.

The right to seek out one's birth parents, or more realistically one's birth mother, was restricted to people over the age of eighteen, it being thought that those younger than that were not emotionally equipped to meet the challenge of coming face to face with those who had given birth to them and who had then stepped out of their lives. But this still represented a considerable number of people, given the scale of children who were put up for adoption until the mid or late 1960s.

The change in the law reflected a huge change in the attitude of society. This change in attitude took two forms— that towards the rights of children generally, and that towards the birth mother, who had in the majority of cases given birth to an illegitimate child.

The later decades of the twentieth century have had their faults, but at least, in stark comparison to the early decades, they have shown some compassion and understanding of the needs of children and some realization that they have rights as people. Things are far from perfect even now, when many children are physically, mentally or sexually abused and when children can be taken over by groups of paedophiles for their own perverted amusement, but at least children are now listened to. For example, children's telephone helplines have been set up to provide a sympathetic ear for children and to provide advice and support for them.

Such help is a very new thing. In the early years of the century children were to be seen—as rarely as possible—and not heard. This was, of course, more the philosophy of the upper and middle classes. Parents in aristocratic and well-off families hardly ever saw their children, except possibly for a few minutes before bedtime, when there was certainly neither the time nor desire to discuss the children's day or to talk over any problems that they might have. Apart from this brief daily sight of their mothers, possibly even fathers, the children were brought up by nannies and maids, who were probably too busy to take much cognizance of what the children were saying and who had doubtless had the adage about children being seen and not heard drilled into them.

The poorer classes could not be exempt from criticism, although they had more excuse for their behaviour. Their children might be seen more often, and even heard, but few people listened to what they had to say, even although poor children grew up much faster than their wealthier peers and were often making a contribution to the upkeep of the family at a distressingly early age, often in distressingly terrible employment conditions.

In the mid–1920s, when a law legalizing and legislating

for adoption was passed, the rights of children were certainly not an issue, because, as has been described above, they were regarded more or less as non-people. Neither were the rights of the birth mother, a term that of course had not then been coined. Of supreme importance were the rights of the adoptive couple, who were generously, in the eyes of the law and society, giving a home to a hapless child. Although infertility in those days did not achieve the attention that it does today, and indeed might not for various reasons have been so prevalent, it was very much a fact of life. There was a class factor in many adoptions, which gave the advantage to the adoptive parents, many of whom were well off and many of whom adopted children from birth mothers in much poorer circumstances. This class factor lessened the rights of adopted child and birth mother even further.

The attitude of the law and society generally has to be seen in the light of the conventions of the day. Until at least the mid–1960s in Britain there was a terrible stigma against being illegitimate. Women who became pregnant outside wedlock were generally reviled and often disowned by their families if the birth fathers could not be persuaded, or forced, to marry them—the solution that was considered most ideal by at least the pregnant women's families, but a solution that often had many barriers in the way.

If this supposed happy ending could not be achieved because the man was already married, because he absolutely refused to marry the woman and ran away or was safely despatched by his family elsewhere, or because the woman either did not know or did not wish to reveal the identity of the father, other means were sought to get rid of the evidence of shame. Some of the women were quite literally thrown out on the streets. At best they were despatched for the duration of the pregnancy to a member of the family or friend of the family living at a distance, from which far place no breath of scandal could affect the family home. In due course, some plausible excuse having been thought up to account for their absence, they returned home babyless, suitable arrangements having been made, doubtless without their consent. Others were consigned to some form of institution for the last part of the pregnancy, from the time when it became physically obvious, and the birth. Conditions in such institutions were often Spartan and virtually intolerable, the pregnant women being made to do hard physical work while also being made to feel extremely guilty and wicked.

Wherever the pregnant woman went, the end result was usually much the same. The baby was taken away, with no regard for the feelings of the birth mother. No one bothered about the bonding process between mother and baby, and the birth mother was allowed to keep the baby simply as long as was necessary for its health, no matter that, by the end of this time, she probably desperately wanted to keep it, whatever her pre-birth views had been. Her views were not consulted, and everyone else knew what was best for her and for the baby. She was expected to give the baby up and advised to put the whole thing behind her and start her life over again with no thought for the child. Frequently she would be treated to a homily on how lucky she had been, despite the magnitude of her shame and guilt.

For the most part it was quite unthinkable that the baby should be kept by the mother. The common solution was adoption. Sometimes the adoption was arranged privately by a family member who personally knew of a couple who had a desperate desire for a baby, and sometimes it was arranged by an adoption society.

Quite often, particularly in the families of the lower echelons, the mother of the family of which the new mother was a member simply took over the child as her own, saying that the child was the result of a late pregnancy. Since we are here referring to a period earlier in the century when pregnancy was a state to be hidden, there were few people brave enough to challenge this statement, least of all the new mother, who was supposed to be duly grateful for having the disgrace of being an illegitimate mother removed from her. It was not necessarily the mother of the new mother who took over the child as her own; it could have been an elder sister who had no children of her own or who was willing to extend her family, or a cousin in similar circumstances.

In the case of family adoptions in villages and small towns where everyone knew everyone else's business, the adoption was often not a particularly well-kept secret, and eventually practically everyone but the child would know who the birth mother was. Given the efficiency of the grapevine in such situations, eventually the child was also informed, although he or she might have been disposed to disbelieve or shut out such information. The particular problems of adopted children who became members of their own families is described later in the chapter.

In the case of formal, non-family adoptions, the only concern seems to have been for the adoptive parents, who were allowed to adopt the baby in total secrecy. The less that was known about the true facts of the birth, the more likely the adoptive parents would be able to bring the baby up as their own. The baby in question was given a brand-new identity, with a brand-new name and a brand-new birth certificate, and as far as the authorities and society were concerned, he or she was starting life all over again with a blank slate.

The idea that children had a right to know about their background simply did not occur to the powers that be. It was assumed that if and when they discovered that they were adopted, they should be suitably grateful to their adoptive parents for bringing them up and would display no interest in their real parents. After all, that was a past chapter in their lives.

Sometimes a child's background might become an issue in his or her relationship with the adoptive parents. If the child was naughty, or committed some kind of misdeed or offence, and the parents knew enough about the birth parents to know that they had been rather wild or guilty of wrongdoing rather than just bringing an illegitimate child into the world, this fact might be cast up to the child by an adoptive parent in a rage—some allusion to bad blood, perhaps. Frequently, however, the child would not understand the allusion, or the adoptive parent, when in a calmer frame of mind, would backtrack and say that he or she had not meant what was said, or that what was said had been misinterpreted. The veil of secrecy and silence, lifted briefly, was soon replaced as securely as ever.

People who, when they grew up, feel a great need to find their birth parents may feel a great sense of resentment that they were given away to strangers, but the whole adoption scene must be seen against the social background of the times. It has to be borne in mind that those were the days before the contraceptive pill became available—even in the mid-1960s it was often difficult to have it prescribed unless one was married or about to be married—and before other forms of contraception became more reliable and more readily available. There were early forms of the sheath or condom around, but, unlike today, people could not simply walk into a chemist and select a packet from the counter, let alone from any other source. The subject of sheaths was an embarrassing one, and tales still abound of how barbers, who sold them, would say rather archly after the customer's hair was duly cut or his chin duly shaved, 'Anything for the weekend, sir?' meaning did the customer need condoms. It took worries about the effect of the pill on women's health, and later the need for a barrier contraceptive to combat Aids and sexually transmitted diseases, to make the condom readily available in vending machines, and so on, by which time research and improved manufacturing had made it a much more reliable product.

Contraception was thus not readily available, and so pregnancy outside marriage was a much more common state than it is today. Of great importance also was the fact that abortion was illegal—in Britain until the Abortion Act of 1967, when abortion under certain circumstances was legalized, the circumstances being open to variation of interpretation, according to medical opinion. Not only could a woman who had had sex not take a pill beforehand to avoid pregnancy or rush out and buy a morning-after pill but, if conception did take place, she could not go to a doctor to arrange for the abortion of the foetus—if a doctor was found to be performing abortions he was struck off the medical register and quite likely sent to prison.

There were people who performed what are often described as 'backstreet abortions' in exchange for varying amounts of money. Of course, such abortions were highly illegal and, moreover, were often carried out by people, often women, who had no medical training and who worked in extremely unhygienic conditions. Pregnant women and girls who consulted such people often died or became seriously ill or permanently infertile. Frequently the illegal abortion operation did not work. Since the whole process was prohibited by law there was little prospect of bringing the illegal abortionist to book, whatever happened.

Women who consulted such illegal abortionist were of course desperate, probably even thinking that death was preferable to giving birth to an illegitimate child. Some had had great difficulty in scraping together the requisite amount of money, sometimes being helped by the baby's father, sometimes even resorting to stealing. Others had no possibility whatsoever of laying their hands on such money and probably would not have known where to find an illegal abortionist anyway. Such people were hardly in a position to advertise their services.

It was common for women, when they realized or suspected that they might be pregnant and before either reluctantly accepting the fact or consulting an illegal abortionist, to try a bit of do-it-yourself abortion. Gin was held to be instrumental in bringing on an abortion or miscarriage, as were very hot baths or falling down from a height. In many cases none of these home remedies for pregnancy actually worked, and the pregnant women were back to square one. Sometimes they injured themselves or the babies in the course of falling.

The circumstances that were prevalent at the time of the birth of many adopted people, who would now be in their fifties, forties or late thirties and who might be searching for, or who might have found, information about their birth parents, have been dwelt on at some length. This is because some understanding of the background of their adoption can give to an adopted person a changed perception of the birth parent who put him or her up for adoption. A knowledge of the social circumstances can make the adopted person less likely to judge the birth parents too harshly. If you simply look at the whole subject of adoption in terms of the social attitudes to pregnancy out of wedlock and illegitimacy in the context of today's attitude, then harsh judgements are all too easy to make.

Basically, earlier in the century the number of babies being born illegitimately and being put up for adoption was greater than the number of couples seeking to adopt, particularly since infertility was either less common or less admitted to. In addition, in the earlier years of the century at least, the expectation of life was considerably less than is now the case, and many more children were left orphaned and put into institutions with possible expectations of being adopted—and of showing due gratitude to those who adopted them.

The pre-mid-1960s' picture was then quite clear. If a baby was on the way to a young woman who was not married and a shotgun wedding or adoption by a family member was equally out of the question, then formal adoption was the only solution. Not only did the family not wish to endure the shame of being related to an unmarried mother but little thought was spared for the child, who, if not adopted, would have to endure the jeers and taunts then doled out to children who were illegitimate.

An illegitimate baby was removed from the mother as soon as possible and handed over to the adoptive parents with as much secrecy and as little information as possible. Everyone was supposed to put the real circumstances of the birth to the back of the mind, except for the fact that some children were told, often when they began to ask about the process of reproduction, that they had been 'chosen' by their parents rather than been 'born' to them. Other children found out by accident, and some presumably never found out. Usually no information about the child's real parents was given, even if this was known, although sometimes it was said, or perhaps implied, that the child's real parents were dead, just for convenience, whether or not this was true. Everyone was meant to live happily ever after.

This veil of secrecy continued until 1975, when the law was changed to allow those who were adopted to have access to their original birth certificates. This change started some people off on a journey to find their real parents and so, some of them must have hoped, to find their real selves. It proved anything but an easy journey, as the search for a birth parent was often long, arduous, time-consuming and expensive. Often, official records, such as marriage and birth registers, had to be gone through, electoral registers and telephone directories laboriously scanned, adoption agencies found and contacted, enquiries made at the last-known address of the birth parent, advertisements placed in newspapers, and so on. Some searches were more arduous than others but few were easy.

The situation was made easier when NORCAP was founded in 1982. This is an acronym for the National Organization for Counselling of Adoptees and Parents, which was set up to help people in their search for birth parents and to counsel them during the search and afterwards. The organization, for example, provides mediators to act as a link between adoptee and birth parent after the parent has been located but before direct contact has been made. It will also put the adoptee in touch with a contact in his or her area, who will give advice and practical assistance. This can save the adoptee much time, effort and expense.

By the 1980s much more attention was being paid to the emotional and side effects of experiences than had been the case earlier in the century. People were aware of the need for counselling after various traumatic incidents in life, and it was recognized that the search for, and particularly the finding of, a birth parent might be very traumatic indeed. Thus it was that those who were adopted before 12 November 1975 were provided with counselling after they had made the decision to seek their birth parents but before they were actually given access to the birth records. Those who were born after that date could choose whether or not to have counselling.

Trying to come to terms with ourselves and seeking out our own identity is difficult enough for most of us to cope with, without having to cope with the discovery that someone from one's early past, who had so much to do with forming our genetic make-up, is in effect a stranger. This genealogical bewilderment adds a whole new dimension to a voyage of self-discovery.

The process of finding a birth parent can sometimes be speeded up for those with sufficient financial resources by employing a professional to do the searching, someone along the lines of a private detective. People with experience in the field of locating and contacting birth parents, however, tend to regard the actual search for the birth parent as an essential part of the process, since the sheer length of the search gives the searcher time to come to terms with the situation and time to consider the various possible outcomes of the end of the search. The search itself can be therapeutic and of psychological importance.

Those whose search for self-discovery also involves the seeking out of a birth parent frequently have yet another problem to contend with. In the shadowy future there might be the discovery of a birth mother, and possibly a birth father, but in the stark present there is the solid presence of adoptive parents, or an adoptive parent, if one of them should be dead.

As has been described above, for the greater part of the century adoptive parents adopted children in an atmosphere of secrecy, the rights of children and birth parents being held to be of no account. Suddenly, in the mid-1970s the situation was changed, and the children, now grown-up, had the right to find out who they really were. Many adoptive parents were devastated and had the feeling that the goalposts had been changed without their consent. Secrecy had been part of their bargain, and suddenly the veils of secrecy had been torn apart.

A sense that they had been betrayed by the establishment was felt by many—after all, they had brought the child up as their own and, as far as they were concerned, they were the true parents—and an even greater sense of betrayal was felt by the adoptees if they instigated searches. This feeling of betrayal and of rejection was sensed by many adopted children, if not actually spelled out to them. Some who truly loved their adoptive parents could not bear to see them being so upset, and either gave up the search for their real parents or never really embarked on it. Who knows at what cost to themselves? Some decided to proceed with the search but left it until the death of their adoptive parents, a decision that often meant that the birth parents also were dead before they could be identified. Their loyalty to their adoptive parents had deprived them of the details of their genetic make-up and true identity.

Others appreciated the feelings of their adoptive parents but felt they had to go on with their quest anyway during the lifetime of their adoptive parents in case they left their search too late. Some felt that they had to undergo the search in secrecy out of regard for the potential feelings of rejection of people whom they loved. Others felt that openness was an essential part of their journey of self-discovery, and either received the reluctant or wholehearted consent of their adoptive parents, or took the risk of falling out with them or of being rejected by them.

When you are looking for something you tend to concentrate all your energies on the search. So it is that many people who were intent on the challenge of finding their birth parents lost sight of the possible outcome of their search. It is at this point that counselling is so valuable. The sheer excitement of meeting one's birth mother, not to mention the relief that the search is at an end, can be such that undue optimism prevails. A counsellor can suggest the potentially negative aspects without pouring too much cold water on the optimism.

Counsellors can gently point out the possibility of disappointment and rejection, and they can quote the details of anonymous but actual cases of this. Birth parents are not always overjoyed at being contacted, either directly or indirectly, by children who may not have been forgotten but who have, by very circumstances, been put to the back of the mind as other aspects of their lives took over.

The worst initial part of the search for birth parents occurs when a birth parent rejects the child. Although it was a social disgrace to have an illegitimate child, many woman who had been in such a situation went on to marry. The birth mother at the time of location is thus highly likely to have a spouse, unless she is a widow or divorcee, and quite possibly another family, the members of which may well know nothing of the half-sibling. The birth parent, particularly a birth mother, like some adoptive parents mentioned above, may feel that the goalposts have been changed to a position not in their favour. Given the veil of secrecy current at the time, they had felt quite secure from the past, and now the past had caught up with them.

She may not have mentioned the fact of having had an illegitimate child, either to her husband or to her new sons and daughters. She may fear loss of face and loss of respect in their eyes and be anxious once again to hush the whole thing up.

Reactions to being contacted by a child who one has put up for adoption earlier in one's life can obviously vary greatly from person to person and from set of circumstances to set of circumstances. Some mothers—it is most often a mother who is contacted first because she is easier to find than the birth father—welcome the arrival into their lives of their long-lost son or daughter, having been half-expecting this since the changing of the law. Others resent the intrusion in their lives, having perhaps been dreading such an intrusion since the changing of the law, and make it quite clear that the son or daughter has no place in her new life.

This latter reaction will obviously have a devastating effect on the adoptee, who has undergone a long and difficult search only to find that the desired goal has not been obtained. True, he or she has tracked down the source of his or her life, which should be of some help in a journey of self-discovery, but to encounter rejection from someone who brought you into the world must be a great blow to the self-esteem and might well leave you wondering what kind of monster gave birth to you. It may well cross your mind that the potential of such cruelty may have been passed on.

Many adopted children who make contact with one or both of their birth parents are quite overwhelmed to discover their close physical resemblance to the parent. In cases of rejection, the feeling of desolation must be even greater if the person who is rejecting you looks very much like you. You have found the source of at least part of your genetic inheritance, but you will be deprived of it again.

Of course, not all mothers who reject the adopted children who contact them are cruel. Sometimes the method of contacting the mother has been too sudden and abrupt so that she has had no time to come to terms with the situation and to examine her own feelings. This is frequently true of the sudden knock at the door approach. If a mediator has been involved, and the approach has been gradual, the chances of a successful reunion are often considerably greater, even in the case of a mother who initially showed reluctance.

As has been mentioned above, some birth mothers have left their husbands and later children in ignorance of the earlier birth. Since it was very probably impressed on her at the time of the birth that it was a source of shame, she may well still feel too ashamed to tell her family the truth, fearing that they will be judgmental of her and that she will lose their respect and love. It may be, in fact, that her husband is rather a sanctimonious person who will be horrified. Perhaps her other children are exceptionally conscious of their social status and feel that the arrival of this illegitimate sister or brother will detract from this status and embarrass them. All the mother can think to do is to get rid of this unwelcome reminder of her shame as soon as possible, although she may feel guilty later.

Other mothers simply cannot cope with the memories of what for them was a very painful experience and may need some kind of therapy before they can cope with this ghost from the past. Their trauma may be heightened if the children whom they had adopted resemble their birth fathers. If the mothers grew to hate or despise the birth fathers, these feelings may well be transferred to their children. On the other hand, if they loved them dearly and had to give them up, then the sight of people looking so like them might open old wounds.

Whatever the reason for the rejection, the very fact of it can have an extremely deleterious effect on the person who is rejected and can affect the rest of his or her life. He or she may experience feelings of worthlessness and find it difficult to establish or continue with relationships. A search to add to self-knowledge that was undertaken with such hope has ended in despair, and a feeling that an insurmountable barrier has been placed in the road to true self-discovery. Worse, there can be feelings that the self is not worth discovering.

People who are rejected at once by birth mothers obviously require counselling or therapy to help them come to terms with what has been for them a double rejection—rejection at birth and rejection on locating their birth mothers. Even more in need of counselling are those who suffer double rejection of a slightly different kind. It is by no means uncommon for a birth mother to welcome her newly returned son or daughter and to create expectations of a warm, long-term relationship, only to reject him or her after a short period. The reasons for this are varied and often highly personal.

Often such late rejection can be a result of the attitude of the mother's husband and later children. They often object to the attention that the new arrival is receiving or his or her presence in their lives may be more a source of embarrassment than they had at first anticipated. Sometimes the mother cannot handle the feelings of guilt, or indeed the feelings of shame, that contact with her once rejected son or daughter brings to her. Sometimes she may find that she does not like the son or daughter, possibly because of a resemblance to the birth father, and sometimes she may simply quickly tire of the relationship, having nothing in common with this reminder of her past.

This second rejection, after a period spent getting to know his or her true mother, is likely to have a traumatic effect on the adopted person. It is a bit like being extremely thirsty and being handed a glass of water only to have it dashed from one's hands with no possibility of replacement. This rejection is worse than an immediate one, since the adopted person may well feel that the rejection is due to some fault in himself or herself. The journey of self-discovery may well bring the adopted person to the conclusion that he or she is worthless, and so this particular journey will have been one that would have been better never begun.

Sometimes, of course, the decision not to continue the relationship, either after the initial contact or after a period of getting to know one another, is not just that of the birth mother. It is sometimes a mutual decision, and sometimes it is that of the adopted person alone.

In either event, the adopted person, having had a successful search and having satisfied his or her genealogical inheritance curiosity, might then be in a position to move on with the journey of self-discovery.

Also in this fortunate position, and indeed in a considerably more fortunate position, are those who find their birth mothers—and sometimes also birth fathers—and succeed in establishing a good relationship with them. Some also go on to have a similar good relationship with half-brothers or half-sisters. The realization that they have siblings can enrich some people's journey of self-discovery even more than the reunion with birth parents. A knowledge of what makes the birth parent and siblings tick can significantly add to someone's self-knowledge.

Several other circumstances can have a traumatic effect on an adopted person who has embarked on the search for a birth parent and has reached the end of the search. One of these circumstances is a seemingly happy one. When some adopted people eventually locate their birth mothers they find that they are married to their birth fathers.

To those of us not personally involved, this might at first sight seem cause for celebration, but the adopted people who are involved often feel a sense of resentment as well as rejection. They feel that they were cast aside and yet the people who led to their birth and to their rejection had lived happily together. Of course there may well have been some kind of extenuating circumstances. For example, the parents may, for some reason or other, have had to separate at or before the birth of their child and got together again and married only years later.

Children and birth parents who make contact with each other and find that they live in very different financial circumstances and have very different lifestyles can experience great difficulties and possibly great resentment. Most affected by such resentment are probably children who have been brought up in much poorer circumstances than their birth mothers or fathers have clearly been experiencing—perhaps their adoptive parents hit bad financial times after the adoption, perhaps they were adopted from an institution by people who were already in reduced circumstances. They are likely to feel that they have been deprived of their birthright and to look at their lives in the light of what might have been if they had not been discarded at birth.

More common is the situation in which an adoptee seeking a birth mother finds her to be in a much poorer set of circumstances than those in which the adoptee has been brought up. It was more likely for people who were relatively well off to adopt children outside the family than it was for poor people to do so. The conflict of the classes is bad enough at any time, but it is exceptionally tragic when it occurs between family members. Such a conflict can prevent a satisfactory reunion with a birth parent from taking place.

The son or daughter may find it difficult to relate to someone who has lived in such different circumstances and may even experience some ill-defined feelings of guilt. He or she may feel it is easier not to continue with the relationship. The birth mother—or perhaps the birth father—may feel it equally difficult to relate to this grown-up son or daughter who has made a late appearance in her—or his— life. Adoptee and birth parent may have totally different accents and totally different attitudes to life, as well as totally different lifestyles. The birth parent may feel that he or she, being poor and working-class, or unemployed, would be a source of shame to a middle-class son or daughter and feel that there is no point in continuing with the relationship.

Thus the conflict of class can stand in the way of a long-term relationship of adoptee and birth parent. It can be exacerbated further if there are siblings involved, adoptee and half-brothers or half-sisters feeling completely estranged from each other by financial circumstances.

Another circumstance is more obviously tragic for the adopted person. It occurs when he or she finds at the end of the search that the birth mother, and or father, is dead and that there is thus no possibility of ever getting to know them. For the adopted person that particular stage of the voyage of self-discovery has come to an untimely and unsatisfactory end. There could also be a worry that the circumstances of the death might prove hereditary—the mother might have died of breast cancer or the father of a very early heart attack. This possibility of major illness and possibly premature death is yet another problem for those trying to come to terms with themselves.

A yet more tragic outcome of a search occurs when the searcher finds that a birth parent has committed suicide. Often very little information is known about the circumstances of suicidal death, and this lack is exacerbated by a long lapse of time. The adopted child of someone who has taken his or her own life will thus have to cope with ignorance as well as with a sense of desolation. He or she may well also be burdened with feelings of guilt and worries that the suicide was the result of a mental illness that may be hereditary. A particularly poignant discovery is that the birth mother committed suicide shortly after the birth.

Of course, birth parents, although dead by the time they have been located, need not have died prematurely or in unnatural circumstances but simply in the natural course of things. This is because many people who have been adopted leave it quite late in life before trying to find out about the circumstances of their birth. The law dictates that anyone who is eighteen or older may institute a search, but in fact many people are considerably older before they institute a search.

As has been mentioned above, sometimes adopted people feel that they would be betraying their adoptive parents if they begin to conduct a search for their birth parents during the lifetime of the people who had effectively performed the parental role all their lives. Sometimes they do not feel the need to seek out birth parents until some event occurs that makes them consider their lives generally and give thought to their inner selves and to their identity.

The decision to instigate a search for a birth mother or birth parents is quite often triggered by some important event in one's own life, particularly some event that makes it desirable that one know more about one's self and one's beginnings. Such events include marriage or the birth of a child, but it can also include a bout of serious illness that leaves one wondering about any possible inherited conditions, and frequently includes the death of adoptive parents, which leaves one free to pursue a search for birth parents without causing hurt to people who have brought one up.

References have been made above to the search for birth parents, but the original search is mostly usually for the birth mother, and the search for the birth father needs further information, time and resources. Finding a birth father is so much more difficult than finding a birth mother because only the name and circumstances of the mother need appear on a child's birth certificate. The father, even if known, can remain anonymous and so impossible to trace through the usual channels of official records.

Some adopted people probably start out thinking that once they locate their birth mothers they will acquire some information that will lead them to their birth fathers, but it is rarely that simple. The birth mother may not have had much information about the birth father in the first place, the liaison that led to the birth having been extremely short-lived or even of the one-night-stand variety. Alternatively, birth mother and birth father might have parted in circumstances that left the mother disliking or despising the father—perhaps he was a married man who had led her on and then abandoned her. Her own feelings may be such that she is reluctant for her son or her daughter to get in touch with the father, and, given the circumstances, she may well totally have lost track of him after the birth anyway.

There may be other highly personal reasons as well—
perhaps the birth mother was raped, perhaps the birth
father was held to be socially much inferior to her and so
she is ashamed of him, perhaps the birth father was, on
the other hand, held to be much her social superior, and so
she is afraid to reveal details of the birth and give information that would enable her child to locate the man in question. The birth mother may simply plead ignorance,
whether this is in fact the case. If she reveals the fact that
she knows more than she is telling, for whatever reason,
then her relationship with the son or daughter might well
suffer.

Those intent on finding both birth parents are very likely
to face a long hard slog that may well not prove to be successful or to have a happy ending. Adopted children who
were born as a result of a liaison between their mothers
and servicemen from another country during wartime face
a particular problem. For example, many American servicemen posted to Britain during World War II fathered illegitimate children and then returned to the United States,
either aware or unaware of their fatherhood. Frequently
they fathered more than one child.

Circumstances involving another country make it even
more difficult for someone trying to locate a birth father,
although this fact might be very important in one's search
for self-identity. Another culture may have affected certain aspects of one's inner self without one having been
aware of it. Even the United States, whilst not regarded as
being foreign as a country and not having a totally differ-

ent language from Britain, is a melting-pot of a country with a mixture of a great many cultures.

The sheer extent of the problem of American servicemen has meant that an organization specifically designed to help trace birth fathers with American military connections has been set up, entitled TRACE, an acronym for Transatlantic Children's Enterprise. Adopted people seeking birth fathers known to have been in the American services, as well as using the services of TRACE, sometimes try to speed up their process of discovery by using American search consultants. It is by no means uncommon for their search to be technically successful but for the whole thing to end in disaster in that the American birth fathers, when found, simply do not want to know. Their lifestyles and positions in society are such that the sudden arrival of a British son or daughter would be a source of embarrassment or inconvenience. When they left Britain after the war they might have put all thoughts of the social aspect of their wartime years behind them.

Of course it is not only fathers in other countries that behave like this. Birth fathers in general are less likely than mothers to anticipate being contacted by a lost son or daughter. Knowing that the law had been changed, knowing that information about them was on the birth certificate, and perhaps knowing of the existence of NORCAP, many birth mothers suspected that it was only a matter of time before they were contacted. Birth fathers, however, knowing of their anonymity on birth certificates, perhaps thought that contact from their children was unlikely, not to say impossible, and so they were unprepared when contact was made.

It has been mentioned above that locating birth parents when another country is involved can be particularly difficult. One large group of children who would certainly find the truth of this was a group of British children who were sent to Australia in the 1940s and 1950s, supposedly to be adopted by Australian families, although most of them ended up in children's homes or were practically used as slaves on farms. Many of them were ill-treated, or even sexually abused, and had been sent to Australia because the country, particularly Western Australia, was markedly underpopulated.

The children, many of whom were in children's homes and many of whom came from poor families, who were despatched were often told lies about their family history, being told that they were orphans when in fact their parents had been still alive at the time of their embarking for Australia. Parents who knew that the children were going were told that they would be adopted in Australia and have a much better life there than they ever would in Britain. Many parents, however, were not told that their children were to be despatched to Australia—some had put their children into a children's home only for a short time when times were hard, and on their return to collect the children were told that they had been sent away. Others were told that they had been adopted, but no mention was made of Australia or anywhere overseas.

The scandal of so many children being sent overseas on

their own, and often under false pretences, was brought to light in 1986 by Margaret Humphreys, a social worker from Nottingham, who had established a service called Triangle, which was open to all the members of the adoption triangle—adopted children, birth parents and adoptive parents. Having put an advertisement for the service in a local paper, she received a letter from Australia from a woman in her forties, claiming that she had been put on a boat in England when she was four years old and sent to Australia with a great many other children.

This letter led Margaret Humphreys to investigate, and she uncovered shocking details of an official scheme that had shipped thousands of children alone overseas. Her story is told by her in the book *Empty Cradles*, published in 1994. Many well-known national charities had been involved in the scheme, which seems to have been endorsed by the government, and the child migration scheme had begun long before the 1940s, other countries, such as Canada and South Africa, having also been the recipients of children.

The information that she uncovered and the anguish that she encountered in the course of her research led Margaret Humphreys to set up the Childs Migrant Trust, which was formed to help people who had been victims of the child migration scheme and to try to assist them in their attempts to find parents or other family members in Britain. Obviously, many of the children who had been despatched under the auspices of the scheme felt as adults a great need to find out who they really were, having been root-

less for years. The Trust found itself inundated with pleas
for help and was faced with the Herculean task of sifting
through records in St Catherine's House in London—
more information on the records office is given in the next
chapter, entitled 'Back to one's Roots'.

Before the founding of the Childs Migrant Trust, victims
of the migration scheme found it extremely difficult, indeed more or less impossible, to acquire any information
about their parents or siblings. The organizations that
were involved in the migration scheme were curiously reluctant to divulge any information to the migrant children
when they had grown up and were beginning to try to look
into their own backgrounds, and in many cases the records
seem to have been lost or destroyed. In addition, of
course, the adults who had been migrant children were
thousands of miles away from the country of their birth
and the place where they might have begun to make some
enquiries. Some of them, especially those who had been
older at the time of their despatch to Australia, might have
had enough memories to enable them to start a search, but
few of them had the money to come to Britain to do so.

Many, of course, had not thought of looking for their
parents until Margaret Humphreys started her enquiries,
because they had always been told that they were orphans.
The anguish of such people must have been very hard to
bear when they eventually, with the help of the Childs
Migrant Trust, located their families, only to find that
their parents were dead. Their only hope was to find siblings, and they might have been only children.

The plight of these particular people, who in fact were mostly not adoptees but children who had been sent thousands of miles away to children's homes—or worse—is of course an extreme case. Not many people have so little to go on when looking for their birth parents, and not many people are so far away from potentially helpful records, but the heartbreak of their search and their longing for some kind of genealogical identity, movingly told in *Empty Cradles*, gives us all a very real indication of how people feel when they are rootless and need a fixed point from which to start on a journey of self-discovery.

As has been pointed out, the migrant children represent a distressingly extreme case when it comes to the acquisition of information relating to the birth parents. A group of people much nearer home, however, who also often find it difficult to receive accurate information are those adults who as children were either adopted by other family members or simply brought up by other family members as their own.

For example, the aunt or sister of the mother of the child in question might have been childless or unable to have any more children and so was quite pleased to adopt the child. In addition, it was extremely common, before it became socially acceptable to have a child out of wedlock, for the mother of the girl or woman who had had an illegitimate child to tell people that the child was hers.

Social circumstances in earlier decades of the century were such that this suggestion seemed much more plausible than it would today. Those were the days when couples tended to have large families, contraception between them either being nonexistent or unreliable. Thus, another baby in the family, even one born to someone in her forties, was no great surprise—nowadays many women in their forties have babies, but they are not usually babies who are part of a large family but babies, often destined to be only children, who are born to career women who have delayed having children until their careers are well under way and secure.

They were also the days when pregnancy was not a state to advertise. Pregnant women, after they began to show obvious signs of their condition, either wore very loose clothes that concealed their expanded girth, or stayed out of the public eye as much as possible. Certainly no one bought a maternity bikini. Thus it was quite possible for someone to be pregnant in a socially acceptable way and for the fact not to be known by all but their closest family.

It was relatively easy for someone to pretend to be pregnant and to appear in due course with a new baby, which was not her own but that of a daughter, sister or niece. The young relative would have been packed off to another member of the family who lived at a distance, or even despatched to an institution, to have the baby in secrecy. Some of the neighbours might suspect the true facts, but they were unlikely to say anything straight out, and in any case the situation was such a common one that it often aroused little comment.

In such situations the mother, sister or aunt sometimes officially adopted the child, but in many cases, particularly in cases where the baby was taken over by his or her grandmother, the whole thing was done on an unofficial basis. Often the mother of the baby, especially if she were very young, stayed on in the same house as the baby to whom she had given birth, leading her life as before. She had to get used to being regarded as the child's sister, irrespective of how she felt about the situation. Sometimes the baby's mother went off somewhere else to earn her living, often helping towards the baby's upkeep and returning at intervals to see the child but keeping up the pretence of the false relationship.

Illegitimacy, as has been mentioned above, was regarded as being shameful in the earlier decades of the century. Unmarried mothers were often shunned by society and often stood a lesser chance of being married if the facts were known. It was thus quite common for men to marry women, only to discover later, sometimes by accident, sometimes by design, that a younger member of the woman's family was not in fact her sister or her brother but her child.

The husband in question often found the news quite traumatic, but the child who was the subject of the secrecy and deception was likely to find the news even more traumatic when he or she eventually found out. To think of oneself as bearing a particular relationship to someone and then to find that this is quite a different relationship is likely to be deeply disturbing. Some children seemed gradually to become aware within the family of the true facts of their relationship to the members of the family, perhaps sometimes even knowing without realizing that they did. Others found out that their sisters were really their mothers from people outside the family, from their peers at school, for example, or from neighbours. The more abrupt the revelation, the more traumatic the effect it was likely to have.

People who do not find out the circumstances of their relationships within their family until they have reached adulthood are often especially disturbed by the revelation, feeling a great sense of betrayal. It is as if they are experiencing a crisis of identity, no longer being the people whom they thought they were. They have to embark on a journey of self-rediscovery, rather than one of self-discovery, and such a journey can be extremely complex. For one thing, it can cause ructions within the family and cause trouble that is never resolved. For another, it can lead to the person who has had to accept a change of relationship having to undergo radical counselling or psychotherapy in order to cope with life.

Many adopted people find that the search for their birth parents helps them to know more about themselves. Even if they never establish a satisfactory relationship with their birth mothers or birth fathers, or both, and even if they never achieve their objective at all, they still feel that the whole learning experience has been of value in their quest for their own identity.

So far, the concentration has been on adopted children and their need to find and relate to their birth mothers or birth parents. It is by no means unknown, however, for birth parents to wish to make contact with the children that they were parted from at birth. Mothers in particular often feel a great burden of guilt about giving up their children and wish to make amends to them and to explain the circumstances that led them to make their momentous decisions.

Many mothers of illegitimate children who would now be grown-up and in a position to instigate a search for their birth parents were very young at the time of the birth. Thus, in the closing years of the twentieth century, they will have been of mature years for rather a long time. They may well have gone through the stage of life when people begin questioning things, such as who they are and why they are doing what they are doing and where they are going in their lives, a stage that often occurs during middle age and is sometimes popularly known as the 'middle age crisis'.

The search by an adopted child for a birth parent is difficult enough, but the search for an adopted child by a birth parent is even more difficult. It is particularly difficult if they do not know the name that the child was given on adoption. If they know the date of the adoption order and the date of birth, which most mothers, at least, will know, they can check through the official register of adopted children and order copies of the adoption certificates of likely candidates. They can also join the Natural Parents Support Group, but the level of help is not of the same degree as children seeking birth parents.

The birth parent, most likely to be the birth mother, can

leave details of her address and so on with NORCAP, described above, or with the original adoption agency in the hope that the adopted child will get in touch. Despite the fact that the state of a mother who has given up a child to whom she has given birth is likely to be at least emotional and perhaps, even years later, in a state of mourning or repressed mourning, there is no compulsory counselling for birth mothers of adopted children. However, a birth mother embarking on a search to find an adopted child would do well to seek out a counsellor, if only to act as mediator if the adopted child is found.

It is unusual for birth fathers to instigate a search for an adopted child. This does not always betoken a lack of regard on the part of the father. It points more to the fact that the role of the father in former times was not as great as it sometimes is today. Paternity leave is at least something that is now talked about; in the earlier decades of the century, when man was the breadwinner and woman the homemaker, it was unheard of.

There are also other reasons for a birth father not instigating a child search. One is the obvious reason that he did not know about the birth, or even of the conception, although he would obviously have been aware of the possibility of conception. Another is that he had even less information to go on than the birth mother and so might well have deemed the search to be unlikely to achieve its aim and therefore not worth embarking on. Yet another cause for reticence, setting aside the obvious ones of lack of concern or of sheer idleness, is that the birth father had the feeling that it was better to let things be and not to interfere with the past.

Not all birth fathers feel like this. Some of them feel, in the way of some birth mothers, that they have reached a stage in their lives when they want to come to terms with who they are. This may involve the need to find any adopted children whom they had fathered. The need may arise from latent paternal feelings, from a burden of guilt, or from a wish to make up to sons or daughters for past omissions.

As has been indicated above, birth mothers, given the circumstances of the availability of information, find it much more difficult to locate children who have been adopted than adopted children do to locate birth mothers. Birth fathers, however, are likely to face the greatest difficulty of all. They may have so little information that they might well not know the date of birth, the date of adoption, or the name of the relevant adoption society, information that birth mothers are likely to have. They have to be very determined to succeed, and they have to have considerable amounts of time, and possibly money, at their disposal in order to pursue their search, for they may have to seek professional help in their quest.

In common with birth mothers, birth fathers have to face the likelihood of a great deal of trauma if they succeed in locating children who have been adopted. They are likely to have to work even harder than birth mothers to establish a relationship and find that the adopted children often blame them for their discarding of their mothers as well as for their discarding of their children. This can be the case whether or not the father was in any way responsible for the adoption.

Thus adoptees and birth parents both face problems when they seek to find each other, and many find these problems too arduous and give up. Often, however, the search has not been completely in vain since the people involved discover something about themselves in the process of the search. Others have some kind of unsuccessful end to their search—perhaps the birth mothers of adoptees have died before they could be located, or perhaps birth parents do not wish to have anything to do with their children, but again the actual search, and even the unhappy outcome, often adds another dimension to the self-knowledge of the searchers. The truly fortunate ones are those who bring their search to a successful conclusion and go on to establish a good relationship with their rediscovered parents, siblings or children. By so doing they can start considering their inner selves in the light of a great deal of new knowledge.

People who have been adopted may actually have as close an acquaintanceship with their inner selves as any of the rest of us do, even before their search. Many of them, however, feel that part of them is missing and that they must do their best to find this missing part. Only then will some of them feel that they are in touch with their true selves.

Chapter 6

Back to One's Roots

Many of us who are not adopted and have maintained relatively regular contact with our parents and most close family members still feel the need to know something about our early beginnings. Instigating a search into our family history can be a rewarding stage in our journey of self-discovery, as a successful search will help us fix our family's place in history, however modest this place may be, and give us an extended idea of our identity. It will also help us to find out how we came to be what we are today, telling us something about the influences that have shaped us.

A search for one's early beginnings can be a difficult one, especially if we want to search far back in the history of our family. It can involve much of the routine work necessary to uncover a birth parent, and it can bring with it the hope and joy, setback and disappointment that a parent search can entail. However, research into family history rarely involves the personal emotional trauma that a search for a birth parent does. One may be disappointed to discover that the members of one's family are not quite as illustrious as one had thought, one might even discover a few guilty or shameful secrets but, unless there are very exceptional circumstances, the disappointments that the family history researcher encounters are the kind that can be taken in one's stride rather than the kind that has a devastating effect on the rest of his or her life.

There are people who, for deeply personal reasons that will vary greatly from person to person, have a compelling emotional need to research their past. However, most of us regard family history research more as a fascinating interest that will add another dimension to our lives and tell us more about ourselves than as a task we absolutely have to undertake. It is certainly an area of research to be considered by people wishing to know the forces that shaped them into being the people they are today.

The last few decades of the twentieth century have seen a tremendous surge of interest in family history. Record offices and libraries report an extraordinary increase in the number of people seeking information on their ancestors. In addition, a great many family history societies have sprung up all over the country while local adult education departments are providing more and more courses to help the family history enthusiast get started on the ancestor quest.

The reasons for this extraordinary increase of interest in our ancestors are varied. There is certainly an element of nostalgia in it. All of us are guilty at some time or other of speaking of 'the good old days', although distance will undoubtedly have lent enchantment to such days; in reality the past had as many problems as the present, just different ones. This reality, however, does not prevent us having romantic notions about the past, and this nostalgia certainly motivates some family history researchers.

It has been mentioned earlier in the book that the later decades of the twentieth century, although for some people at least decades of affluence, have been, for many, decades of insecurity. Much of this insecurity had its roots in high unemployment rates and the ever-present threat of redundancy. There is no doubt that this kind of insecurity has given some people a desire to look for some sense of security in history. Finding out more about their roots they feel, very possibly unconsciously, would provide an increased sense of security in broader terms.

Added to this sense of insecurity in many people has been a deep feeling of dissatisfaction with the ultra-swift pace of change of the later decades of the twentieth century, particularly the pace of technological change. It is this feeling of dissatisfaction, often allied with a sense that the world is becoming far too materialistic a place, that has made several people, often quite affluent people, decide to abandon their lifestyles and to go and live a much simpler, less technological and less materialistic life in a remote, or relatively remote, rural area, often in the north of Scotland but sometimes abroad, as in parts of rural France. The same feelings have motivated the New Age travellers in the 1990s, who travel round the country in groups and try to camp on what they feel is common ground.

This dissatisfaction with the hectic urban life may also

be a factor in the increase of interest in family history.
People who feel that they do not care for the speed and so-
phistication of modern life may feel drawn to a more simple life and may express, possibly unconsciously, this at-
traction by exploring their early history in times when
they assume simple lives prevailed.

As has been pointed out, the reasons for the surge of interest in family history are varied. Yet another contribu-
tory factor is likely to be related to the interest in conservation and preservation that has arisen in the later decades
of the twentieth century. Many people became concerned
about the environment and the damage that was being
done to it by many of our twentieth-century inventions.

Just as people were expressing concern for the rain for-
ests and the ozone layer, and trying to prevent further
damage to them, so some people have become concerned
that details of a vanishing way of life are being lost. Thus,
research is being undertaken by universities and other
bodies to collect information, for example, on old village
customs that were in danger of dying out with the deaths
of the old people in a village. Another area of interest is
the capturing on tape of dialect words and expressions
from old people before they died.

This concern for conservation and preservation, especially those aspects that are related to the preservation for
posterity of details of customs and language, is very likely
to have sparked off an interest in family history. An interest in one's own family history is an obvious offshoot of a
general interest in local history.

There are more practical reasons for the current passion
for tracing one's family tree. One of these is that people in
the later decades of the twentieth century often have more
leisure than they did in earlier years, although the 1990s
are seeing more and more people working very long hours
in order to keep their jobs. Those who have increased leisure do so partly because labour-saving devices in the
home leave us more time, but the increased leisure can be
the result of having to take very early retirement as a form
of redundancy, or it can be the result of being unemployed. Whatever the reason for the leisure, it is a fact that
more people have more hours to fill, and they turn to hobbies to help them do so.

Not all of us, particularly older people, are seeking a
hobby connected with the keep-fit preoccupation of the
later decades of the twentieth century. Squash, working
out at the gym and weight-training are all very well for
some, but many people with increased, or enforced, leisure are older and are looking for a more sedentary area of
interest. Research into family history can be just the interest that such people are looking for. It can involve travel,
particularly if one has come from a rather mobile family,
but much of the initial research can be done from records.

The age at which people develop an interest in their family history varies greatly, as does the personal reason for
the initiation of the research. For example, a young man in
his early thirties who has just become a father may suddenly feel the need to find out more about the family of
which his son or daughter has just become a member.

On the other hand, the kind of increased leisure that comes as a result of one's age often also comes at a time when one is beginning to reflect on one's life and what one has done during it. Such reflection can easily be accompanied by a desire to know how we have come to be what we are and what influences have shaped us, not only physically but also with regard to character, personality and disposition. To satisfy such a desire one must look to the past, and thus another amateur family historian is born.

Another practical reason for the increase in interest in family history is simply that it is now much easier to trace one's ancestors. Record offices are now much more approachable places and allow members of the public access to original sources, often also providing trained staff to offer guidance and advice. The advent of microfilm, microfiche and computers has made the task easier, after the searcher has got over the initial reticence to use them.

Furthermore, we live in an age when much more information is available to the ordinary person than it ever was before. If you want advice on how to set about the task of tracking down your ancestors, it comes in several forms. There is a host of information books providing the know-how on how to tackle a wide range of subjects, and there has been a marked increase in the diversity of adult education classes run by local authorities, universities or colleges. Basically, if you want to do something you can almost certainly find out how to do it without too much trouble.

The single most difficult hurdle you are likely to have to

overcome in your search for your forebears is that of inertia. Most of us at some time or other have probably toyed
with the idea of embarking on research into family history
but it is all too easy to think that one would never find the
time or the energy, while slumped in front of the television watching something that you probably do not want to
watch anyway. Instead of getting started on the search,
many of us simply push the idea to the back of our minds
and never do get started.

Sometimes it is not simply inertia that holds us back but
a lack of knowledge of how to set about beginning the
search. As has been indicated above, there is, in fact,
plenty of information available to you, but you might very
well not know that. Then there is the fact that many people
would be nervous of entering a records office and nervous
about asking for help on how to make use of the records. It
is also all to easy to be put off by the evidence of new
technology around you in records offices and libraries,
and to feel daunted by the thought of having to use a microfilm reader, for example.

Once you have safely negotiated these potential barriers
and have got your search under way, you may well find
that it is difficult to force yourself to take time off from it.
Family history can very easily become a consuming passion, rather than just a hobby, as it becomes more and
more absorbing. Some amateur family historians stop after constructing a pedigree and compiling a family tree,
but others get bitten by the history bug and try to flesh out
the bare bones of the family tree with information regard-

ing the lifestyles of their individual ancestors and the places in which they lived. They even go on to have an interest in history generally, both local and national, as well as their family history

That is all very well, you may ask, but how do you get started? First of all, it is a very good idea to check and see if there is an adult education course on the subject in your area and sign up for it if there is. If there is not, then you could suggest that such a course is put on the curriculum for the following session. Such a course will give you confidence, knowing that you have the basic knowledge required to embark on your search.

It is also a good idea to check at your local library to see if there is in existence a family history society in your area. Recently, many of these have sprung up all over the country, and if you find that there is not such a society locally you might think about starting one up. Not only can such societies help by the exchange of information and techniques among members, but they can also prevent one giving up one's search too easily. The members of a society like this are often extremely enthusiastic about their hobby, and other people's enthusiasm can be infectious when one's own is fading. Most local family history societies belong to the Federation of Family History Societies, a national organization that publishes useful, inexpensive guides and its own magazine, *Family History News and Digest*. Some local societies produce their own journals and publish editions of local records, such as census returns.

In the absence of such local help, you should take yourself off to your local library or your local bookshops. You will almost certainly find a book that provides enough information to get you started on your quest. A word of warning is necessary before you begin. Try not to have too high expectations of the kind of ancestor whom you are likely to uncover. The chances of revealing a famous aristocrat are remote, so if you have been glamorizing your historical roots now is the time to be a bit more realistic.

Most people, unless they are adopted, know at least something about their family's past, even if this past is fairly recent. Before you go hunting around in record offices and libraries, it is extremely useful to assess what you can find at home or from other family members. It is a source of sadness that many people do not develop an interest, or at least do not activate an interest, in family history until they are middle-aged or even elderly. This means that they have lost the opportunity of finding out first-hand information from older members of their own family, who will be dead by the time the search for information is instigated. In fact, the best time to start at least relatively recent family history research is when you are still at school and when many of your relatives are still alive. Bearing this in mind, some schools set family history research as a school project

Anyone who does have any older family members still alive should start with them. It is important to take along a notebook, or even a tape recorder—although some older interviewees might be put off by this—to record the infor-nation in a systematic way rather than rely on one's memory. It is also important to go along determined to be patient, especially if the person to be interviewed is quite old. The topic of family history easily lends itself to a discursive approach. Many old people become extremely garrulous and nostalgic when they start talking about old times and frequently digress onto issues that are not really related to family history research and so do not get the amateur historian any further forward. If the mental faculties of the old person concerned are not as sharp as they were, the information provided can be very confusing.

Indeed, it is important right at the beginning of the research to be scrupulous about taking notes and about trying to systematize the material as far as possible as you go along. Rough notes may be seem all very well at the beginning, but scrappy material is difficult to interpret later, although it seems perfectly comprehensible at the time of writing. In any case, in hardly any time at all the researcher will have information relating to more than one branch of the family, and a degree of organization, such as the use of a separate notebook for each separate family branch, becomes necessary. In these days when many people have home computers or word processors many researchers prefer to store their findings electronically, although unless they have laptop computers they usually take notes as they go along and type their findings up later. It really does not matter how you choose to organize and store your material as long as you have some form of reasonably flexible system and as long as you are careful always to follow it. Otherwise much of your valuable work may be wasted.

As information is gathered on the various branches of the family, it will become necessary to construct some form of family tree. It is difficult to give hard and fast rules about the method of displaying family tree material. For one thing, the number of children varies greatly from family to family and from generation to generation. A few general comments, however, might prove helpful.

It is best for purposes of clarity not to try to put too much material on any one sheet of paper but to use a different sheet of paper for each branch of the family. To some extent the method of displaying the material depends on what you want it for. For example, if you want to demonstrate a line of descent clearly for ease of reference then a very bare outline of the essentials on one sheet of paper is what is required. It is useful to list people who are of the same generation at the same level on the page and to list husband and wife beside each other. Basically, the researcher will work out a system that suits him or her in the course of the research.

Since abbreviations are a necessary part of family trees it is sensible to use those abbreviations that are standard in genealogy. Some of these are listed below for guidance—whether you use a full stop or not is now often considered to be a matter of preference.

b. born
bpt. baptised
d. died

d. unm. died unmarried

d.s.p. died without children (Latin *decessit sine prole*)

dau. daughter

s. son

div. divorced

unm. unmarried

= married

l left descendants

Not only notebooks and computers are useful adjuncts to family research. As has been indicated above, a tape recorder can also be very useful. The advantage of taking along a tape recorder when gathering oral information is that you can record the whole conversation and then listen to it carefully at your leisure, several times if necessary. Even if you felt at the time of the interview that nothing worth recording was said, you might easily find that in among all the seemingly unimportant rambling are some useful facts or leads that you failed to notice at the time. You might, for example, find out the occupation of a family member or the birthplace of another one, and so on.

The family researcher interviewing an old or elderly person, or, for that matter, any member of the family, on the subject of family history should proceed with caution and a certain degree of scepticism as well as patience. Every family has its share of family folk tales that are more likely to be based on fantasy rather than on fact. Tales of romantic family figures illegitimately descended from a royal family are almost certainly apocryphal, however an established part of family folklore they are.

Most families, or at least some branches of them, move around to a greater or lesser degree. Thus, the serious family researcher intent on getting as much information as possible at first-hand from relatives may have to be prepared to travel. This could prove time-consuming and expensive, especially if some family members have moved abroad, and in fact may prove impossible because of this.

It is obviously sensible to start with those sources that are close to home. Having talked to older members of the family, it is often useful to talk to older neighbours, if the area is one where people do not tend to move around much. If you live in a small town or village, where again the level of mobility has been small, it is also worth trying to talk to some of the older local residents to see if they know anything about any of your ancestors. Of course, caution and scepticism are again to be recommended, as much that is passed on may simply be gossip. Still, when the tape recording is played over the researcher may find that a few valuable nuggets of information have been acquired or at lest a valuable lead given

When all the oral sources have been exhausted, the amateur family historian should turn his or her attention to family photographic or written sources. If travel has been involved in the acquiring of the oral sources it is as well to find out before leaving if the person in question has any family photographs, family records, such as birth and marriage certificates, letters, and newspaper cuttings. If she or he does, the researcher can photocopy them and return them in case any other family member has need of them at any point. It is disturbingly easy for things to get lost when people borrow them.

The amount of information to be gathered from photographic and written sources varies greatly from family to family. Some families are more apt to take photographs than others, although obviously this can change from generation to generation. Some were more likely to write letters than others—nowadays, because of the telephone, far fewer personal letters are written—and some were in situations where there was more likely to be an exchange of letters between family members. For example, those with family members in the forces, or those with family members who had gone abroad to live, would be more likely to write and receive a lot of letters than others.

How much informal family memorabilia there is often depends on whether the family consists of hoarders or not, or on how much space there was to hoard things. The hoarder is a family researcher's dream, but it takes just one obsessively tidy family member with no regard for old things to deprive a family of much valuable information. Moving house is often an unfortunate time for family memorabilia, as this exercise often involves throwing out large quantities of stuff. A family that has not moved around much and has a reasonable amount of storage space, for example in attics, is the most likely to have photographs, letters and newspaper cuttings to consult—a treasure trove for family researchers.

Photographs can be a source of frustration since they are frequently unlabelled, having been stuck in a drawer somewhere rather than pasted in an album with the names, dates and occasions tabulated. If, in fact, the photographs have been pasted up and labelled then this is indeed an extra bonus for the researcher. Frequently, however, photographs, even if unmarked and seemingly valueless in themselves, are a useful lead-in to an interview with an old person. These often stir his or her memory or interest, and of course light may be thrown on the identity of the person in the photograph.

Family birth, marriage and death certificates are obviously of great help to the family researcher. Although these can be found in the record office, locating them within the family at least saves a stage in the process and can speed up the search. Be prepared to find a few skeletons in the family cupboard if you are looking through old family certificates. It is often in the course of this procedure that someone finds that a family member has been born illegitimate, another has been adopted, parents have never been married, and so on. Finding such secrets is almost an inevitable consequence of digging up the past.

Newspaper cuttings can also be a valuable source of family information. Often these take the form of birth, marriage and death announcements, valuable in themselves, but they can also relate to the activities of family members in the community. These activities can cover many fields and might give some indication as to the status of the family in the community. For example, an uncle might have been mayor, a cousin might have won a medal for bravery, a great-uncle might have done exceptionally well at school, a great-aunt might have died in an accident, a distant relative might have been an actor, yet another relative might have ended up in jail for fraud, and so on.

Letters can be the most interesting form of family memorabilia, since they can shed so much light not only on family members and relationships but also on social conditions of the time. Sadly, these are often the least likely family documents to survive, being regarded as a load of rubbish by someone intent on having a good clearout or having been destroyed by the receiver before his or her death. This is extremely unfortunate since many people did actually keep collections of letters—lovers, for example, or a mother with a son in the army or a daughter in domestic service. Preserved letters are extremely interesting and often of great value to the family historian, but they can be extremely difficult to read. They may be in very poor condition, the ink may be very faded, and the writing may be practically illegible. Still, the perseverance and effort required may well prove worth it.

The next step in family history research may seem rather macabre. It is a visit to the graveyard. Even if you know exactly where a particular ancestor died, this is not always an easy task. The oldest tombstones date from the seventeenth century, and many, even relatively modern ones, are in a very poor state, to the extent that some of them have been removed. When they are crumbling and worn practically smooth they are difficult to interpret.

Originally graveyards were attached to churches, and in

some rural areas these are still in use. However, in the course of time churchyards, particularly in cities and large towns, became too full and could not cope with the demand. An alternative solution had to be found. Thus, in 1827 the first public cemetery was opened in London at Kensal Green, and in 1850 an Act of Parliament gave authorization for the General Board of Health to close old churchyards and build cemeteries for burials instead.

Even apart from their crumbling condition, tombstones can cause problems when it comes to interpreting them. Sometimes the tombstones were not erected until a considerable time after the death of the first person to be named on them, and thus the information cannot be held to be reliable. One also has to be careful of ages—for example, if a man died when he was 62, the age he was at his death could be recorded on the tombstone as 63, since he was regarded as being in his 63rd year.

If the ancestor about whom information is being sought was buried in a public cemetery you might find that the relevant records are still located at the office situated at the cemetery, rather than being deposited in the local record office, and can be consulted there. The information available there is arranged chronologically, not alphabetically, and so the family researcher is more likely to have success if he or she has some idea of the date of death. The cemetery records usually give the name, address, age and occupation of the person buried and also record the date of death, the date of burial and the location of the grave in the cemetery.

Having noted and mulled over as much information as possible from the sources mentioned above, the family researcher is ready to embark on the task of tackling the record office. Even if the research to date has been fairly fruitless, the researcher will not have wasted time. At the very least his or her resolve will have been tested—the fainthearted will have already given up. He or she will also have gathered confidence and some knowledge as to how to proceed further.

A degree of confidence is necessary to enter a record office and begin the search. Details of the location of the nearest office can be had either from the local library or from the local telephone directory, and admission to a record is usually free. Record offices employ professional archivists to categorize and take care of the material stored there. They are usually willing to give some guidance to people engaged on family history research, but they have a great deal of other work to do and so you must not expect them to do your research for you. They are far more likely to be helpful to you if you have some idea of what you are looking for and if you have at least tried to make some progress on your own. Presumably they are all too used to encountering helpless people who are virtually looking for an unpaid researcher.

Registration certificates—England and Wales

In England and Wales the system by which births, marriages and deaths had to be registered began in 1837. The indexes relating to the registration of such family events from that date are located at the General Register Office, St Catherine's House, in Kingsway in London. The material is available for consultation, there is no admission charge, and you do not have to make an appointment.

Formal situations are often rather daunting until you get used to them, and this is true of record-searching at St Catherine's House. The indexes to the births, marriages and deaths are arranged on shelves with a separate section for each, the sections being arranged chronologically up to the present time. The various years are divided into quarters, labelled respectively March, June, September and December, and the surnames are arranged alphabetically within each quarter. If the researcher does not know the exact date of birth but knows roughly the year it will take slightly longer, but he or she will very likely find the relevant entry with persistence. It also must be taken into consideration that births were not always registered right away. From 1984 the indexes are compiled for the full year.

As has been indicated above, the surnames of the entries are listed alphabetically within each quarter. Then, the forenames are arranged alphabetically under each surname—the fashion for having more than one forename did not come into being until some time after the introduction of official registration. In addition, from 1911 the maiden name of the mother is also given. Also given in the index is the name of the Superintendent Registrar's District where the birth was registered.

Books indicating the location of these registration dis-

tricts are available at the front desk of the General Register Office at St Catherine's House, or you can obtain from
the Society of Genealogists a booklet by Ray Wiggins entitled *St Catherine's House Districts*. This contains an al-
phabetical list of the original districts, around 650. Registration districts are more complicated than you might
think, and they are quite large in extent, considerably
larger than parishes. A knowledge of which registration
districts you are likely to be interested in could save you
time and effort when consulting the indexes. Knowing the
registration district narrows the range of the enquiry.

If you simply want to confirm the existence or rough
date of birth of an ancestor then your search might end
with the index. If, however, you want to see a copy of the
relevant certificate in case, for example, it divulges more
information to speed you on your search, then you will
have to fill in an application form, pay a fee—consulting
the indexes is free—and either collect the certificate after
a few days or have it sent it you.

It is worth pointing out that you should try to be as sure
as possible that you have struck gold before ordering the
certificate. If you adopt a more hit-or-miss approach and
order several certificates, you can soon incur quite a lot of
expense, particularly if you are seeking information on
several ancestors.

The more accurate information that you have about your
ancestor, the more likely you will be to get quick results,
but some searches can take a lot of time and effort.
Margaret Humphreys, who uncovered the scandal of Brit-

ish children being sent to Australia, Canada and other overseas countries, describes in her book *Empty Cradles*, which deals with the plight of the migrant children and their anguished attempts to find their parents, the amount of time and effort required for some searches and the sheer weariness and despair that can accompany an unsuccessful search.

Since the family historian is not trying to locate a parent, with the possibility that he or she is either dead or might die before the search is successful and contact made, but simply an ancestor, probably known to be dead, a long search is unlikely to produce actual despair or trauma, but it can easily induce weariness. Apart from anything else, the sheer bulk of the indexes can make the task physically tiring.

It is often difficult to be sure that you have located the correct entry in the indexes, particularly if you are not completely sure about the date and have either not thought about the problem of registration districts or do not know which is the relevant one. The problem is exacerbated if the person whose birth details you are seeking has a very common name, particularly if he or she was born before the time when the fashion for giving a child more than one forename.

To take extreme examples, imagine locating John Smith or Mary Jones. Even the addition of another forename does not always help. There must, for example, be a considerable number of people over the years who were named John James Smith or Mary Anne Jones, or any number of combinations of common names, bearing in mind that the fashion for ordinary families to avoid common names is a relatively recent one. Since a person with several forenames, especially if these are relatively unusual, is easier to locate, perhaps we should think of future generations of ancestor-hunters when we are naming our children.

When you have survived the toils of the search and received the correct birth certificate for your ancestor, you are ready to move on to the next stage, or rather to go back in time one stage further. Much information is to be gleaned from a birth certificate, in that it records the day, month and year of birth, the place of birth, the name and sex of the person in question, the forename/forenames and surname of the father—although this can be left blank if the child is illegitimate—the forename/forenames, surname and maiden name of the mother, the occupation of the father, and the name and place of residence of the person who supplied the information, 'the informant'—often the father.

Armed with this knowledge it is back to the indexes for more information, it being time to try to locate the marriage particulars of your ancestor's parents. In the marriage indexes bride and groom are listed separately, which of course increases your chances of locating details of their marriage. If both parents had very common names and had married a considerable amount of time before the birth of your ancestor—perhaps your ancestor was the youngest of a very large family—finding the date of their marriage and so locating their marriage certificate can mean another long struggle with the indexes.

As has been mentioned above, from September 1911 the mother's maiden name appears on a birth certificate and so you have the choice of beginning with either her or the father. The choice may be an easy one to resolve if one surname is much less common than the other one. It is hard luck if your ancestor was the issue of a John Smith and a Mary Jones. Having located what you suspect might be the relevant one, or, as is often the case, located a number of possibilities, you can crosscheck the facts under the name of the other partner in the marriage.

It is, of course, possible that the parents of your ancestor were never married—the absence of a father's name on the birth certificate will have given you an indication of the possibility of this. Of course, the mother of your ancestor may well have married someone else some time after the birth, in which case you will be able to elicit the date of this marriage and the name of her husband. Alternatively, the parents of your ancestor may have for some reason or other been unable to marry before the birth but married each other at a later date. Again details of the marriage will be located in the index.

As well as the date of marriage and the surname and forename/forenames of the relevant party—bride or groom—the entry in the marriage index also indicates the registration district where the marriage ceremony took place. Some information on registration districts is given above under locating birth certificates.

In addition, from 1912 onwards the surname of the bride is recorded on the groom's index entry, and correspondingly the surname of the groom is recorded on the bride's index entry.

When you are reasonably certain that you have located the correct marriage index entry—it becomes easier after 1912, as described above—it is time to seek out the actual marriage certificate. The procedure is the same as it is for obtaining a birth certificate. You fill in the application form, pay the relevant fee, and either collect the certificate or have it sent out to you.

You will find that the details given on the marriage certificate include the name and district of the church or register office where the marriage ceremony took place—register office weddings used to be uncommon, but they have become progressively more common until they now represent the majority since the decrease in church membership; the date (day, month and year) of the marriage ceremony; the forename and surname of the groom; the forename and the surname of the bride; the age of the groom; the age of the bride—many marriage certificates before 1870 do not specify the age but record the fact that the relevant person was 'of full age', a term that does not necessarily indicate the age of 21, the birthday that the phrase 'coming of age' used to mean, or the age of 18, the birthday that the term now signifies, but sometimes simply 'the age of consent', a then unspecified age that, until 1929, might have been even lower than the age of 16; what is described as the 'condition' of the parties involved, that is, whether the groom is a bachelor or a widower, or whether the bride is a spinster or widow; the occupation or 'rank or profession' of the groom and bride respectively; the place of residence of the groom and bride respectively; the forename and surnames of the father of the groom and the father of the bride respectively; the 'rank or profession' of the father of the groom and the father of the bride respectively; the names of the witnesses, whose signatures follow the signatures of the bride and groom, although the signatures, like the signature of the 'informant' on the birth certificate, are not original but copies made by the registrar.

The indexes of deaths in St Catherine's House are also useful sources of information to the family historian. They are categorized in a manner similar to the indexes of births and the indexes of marriages, and after 1866 they include the date of death, although this should be regarded as being approximate, particularly in the case of older people.

A death certificate records the date and place of death; forename/forenames and surname of the deceased; the sex of the deceased; the age of the deceased (see the paragraph above); the occupation of the deceased; the cause of death; the signature, description and place of residence of the person registering the death, 'the informant', who is usually the next kin of the deceased or a close relative or friend.

Sometimes, despite a long and thorough search, you fail to find an entry for someone whom you feel ought to be listed. The most likely explanation is that, for various reasons, your information is not as accurate as you think it is. Another possible explanation is that some clerical error has occurred. For example, the local registrar might have made a mistake in recording the relevant information—not everyone thinks to check such information, and in the early years of civil registration many people were illiterate. Also, not everyone has proofreading skills, and it would be easy for informants, who were very likely in the grip of some emotion, either joy at a birth or a marriage or grief at a death, not to spot an error made by the registrar, of whom they were probably in awe. Further potential for clerical error lay in the fact that the entries were copied into the indexes by an official other than the original registrar. At the very least, the name may have been given an alternative, but wrong in that particular case, spelling. It is worth trying to think what errors might have been made, an initial M for an initial N, and so on, and then to look in the relevant index.

There are various other reasons why you can fail to locate someone whom you feel sure should be listed. One is that the information given was for some reason deliberately false, and another is that the information given was for some reason deliberately and illegally withheld. Moreover, we have to acknowledge the fact that it took quite a while for everyone to become aware of the legal necessity for official registration of births, marriages and deaths, and although official registration of births became law in 1837, it was not until 1875 that parents were penalized for not so doing. Thus, until that date quite a few births went unregistered. There appears also to have been some confusion in parents' minds between registration and baptism, some thinking that if you had a child baptised you did not need to register him or her.

If you find it difficult to travel to St Catherine's House, you can try starting with your local register office. However, in order for this to be of value you have to be already in possession of some accurate information, such as precise dates. Local register offices obviously have the advantage of being easier to reach than St Catherine's House, unless you live in central London, and they are useful places not only to locate the more easily locatable of your ancestors but also to practise your research skills before you tackle General Register House. The local offices do have the disadvantage of not having enough staff to deal with many enquiries and not having enough appropriate facilities. In addition, the indexes in local register offices, unlike those in General Register House, St Catherine's House, are not available for consultation by the public and so you really have to have a good idea of what you are looking for in advance. Even the least mobile of families have moved around quite a bit, and there is little possibility of all branches of a family, and all generations of it, staying within the boundaries of the same register office. Eventually your search will have to take you to the comprehensive and global files of St Catherine's House.

Some people do find the journey to St Catherine's House

difficult, and some find the physical task of coping with the rather cumbersome indexes tiring. The indexes are available on microfilm in some public libraries, the Society of Genealogists, and the Mormon research institutions. You still have to obtain the relevant certificate of birth, marriage or death from St Catherine's House, although the application can be made by post at some expense.

Scotland

What has been said above about St Catherine's House is true only for England and Wales. In Scotland, records relating to births, marriages and deaths are kept at General Register House, New Register House, just off Princes Street in Edinburgh. The national system of registration of births, marriages and deaths did not begin in Scotland until 1855, and there are some differences in the nature of the certificates relating to this registration. The Scottish certificates are fuller, and so more informative. For example, they indicate the date of the marriage of the parents on a birth certificate, the names of both parents of both parties on a marriage certificate, and the names of both parents of the deceased on a death certificate.

Ireland

In Ireland general registration did not start until 1864, although there was some degree of registration of marriages. Registration entries from each county are filed together, but it is more difficult to trace a family line, there being no consolidated index. The registration records for Ireland for the period up to 1922 are kept at the Office of the Registrar General, Joyce House, in Lombard Street in Dublin. Here too are the records for Eire (later the Republic of Ireland) for the period after 1922. Records relating to Northern Ireland are to be found at the General Register House, Oxford House, in Chichester, Belfast.

There has always been a strong link between Ireland and parts of England, such as Liverpool, and between Ireland and parts of Scotland, such as Glasgow. Many Irish people emigrated to England and Scotland, and so many of us may well find that we have to make use of the Irish records at some point.

Census returns

The General Register Offices provide an incredibly rich source of material for the family historian, but there are other sources also—census returns, for example. Although the first census with respect to England and Wales was taken in 1801, and taken every ten years after that, the first one that is really of much value is that of 1841. This is because the General Register Office took over the responsibility for the collection of the census data in 1840, and the whole business of collecting and categorizing the information became more systematic and efficient. There was a separate census taken for Ireland, but in Scotland the census-taking was the responsibility of the Registrar General for Scotland.

It should be noted that the only relevant year (every tenth

when the census was not taken was 1941, which was in the middle of World War II. It should also be noted that the early census returns for Ireland were destroyed when the Public Records Office was destroyed by fire in 1922.

In the 1841 census, the first one to be carried out by the Registrar General's Office and taken in June, the people collecting the census information, called the enumerators, were asked to write down the names of the people in the household or institution. The exact age of each child under the age of 15 in the household or institution was recorded, the exact age of older people was not given, ages being rounded down to the nearest five. Thus, someone who was aged 44 in 1841 would appear as 40 in the census, and someone who was 28 would appear as 25. Also included in the 1841 census was the occupation of people under the heading 'profession, trade, employment or of independent means'. Another question in the 1841 census related to place of birth. Was the person born in the same county of which he or she was currently resident or had he or she been born in Scotland, in Ireland, or in what was described as 'foreign parts'?

The first census organized by the Registrar General's Office required some fine-tuning before the taking of the next census. This fine-tuning, although not of course carried out with the amateur family historian in mind, did improve his or her chances of success.

One important change was the fact that from 1851 onwards exact ages were to be given and the practice of rounding them down was to be abandoned. This, being much more precise, was a considerable improvement for the family historian.

Another important change that improved the lot of those later engaged in establishing family trees was the one that indicated that the exact birthplace should be given rather the much vaguer information previously requested. Another change, and one that was again useful to the family historian, if not quite as useful as the other changes mentioned, was the fact that from 1851 on the relationship of each person in the household to the householder had to be stated.

Only records up to 1891 are available to the public, the rest, as with some other official information, having to remain secret until it is one hundred years old. The census returns up to 1891 are available on microfilm at the Public Record Office in Chancery Lane in London, although they are scheduled to be moved to the Public Record Office at Kew in the relatively near future. Admission is free, although a reader's ticket has to be obtained.

Unlike the indexes relating to births, marriages and deaths, the census indexes do not relate to surname. Instead they relate to place. They are arranged according to the year the census was taken and provide a reference number for each enumerator's district. This helps the researcher to obtain what he or she hopes is the relevant microfilm, that is, the film that relates to the district where his or her ancestor was on the night the census was taken.

If you live far from London you may be able to save yourself a journey, at least in some of the stages of your research. County record offices and the reference libraries in many large towns hold microfilm copies of the census returns relating to the district that the office or library serves.

The census returns, however, cannot be regarded as gospel. The problem relating to age with reference to the 1841 census is mentioned above. Even after the practice of rounding down the age was abandoned, however, there could be problems. There is the obvious one that not everyone always tells the truth, whether to the census enumerator or otherwise. Another is that in the early years at least some people might have had only a rough idea of their age. Also, there could have been a degree of confusion in that some people might have thought that they were being asked for their age next birthday instead of the age they were the previous one.

For whatever reason, it is the case that there are many discrepancies, in that a good proportion of people do not seem to have aged ten years by the time the next census came round. Sometimes this discrepancy amounts to a year or two, but sometimes it amounts to a considerably longer period. The family historian seeking an ancestor, therefore, should not assume that the recorded age is accurate and so assume a birth year, but should assume that the recorded age may be approximate rather than precise, and so assume several possible birth years.

Birthplace entries on censuses can also indicate signs of imprecision and discrepancies. Sometimes such imprecision can be put down to someone deliberately misleading the enumerator by deliberately giving false information, but sometimes also it can be put down to confusion. For example, if you had been born somewhere very small, such as a small village or hamlet, you might have assumed that few people outside it had heard of it, and so you might have put the nearest town. Some people, even nowadays, adopt this policy when asked for their birthplace. This could account for the fact that the birthplace of a person can be different in two succeeding census returns.

It is also quite possible that some people gave the name of the place where they had been brought up as children rather than the place they were actually born, either because they forgot for the moment that they had been born somewhere else and moved shortly after birth or because they had never known that the two places were different. In the case of a large family that had moved around a lot the parents might have misremembered which child was born where. We can but speculate, but family historians should be aware of the problem.

When it comes to information regarding occupation, the family researcher should be aware of the fact that in Victorian times it was common for one person to have more than one job, especially at different times of year. Someone might own a smallholding and also be a craftsman, or someone might be a farmworker in the summer when there was plenty of work around and do something different, such as carpentry, in the winter. These dual occupations are not always indicated in the census returns.

Although there are some problems and discrepancies in

he enumerators' returns, the census returns can be ex-
remely useful to the family researcher. They are at their
nost valuable as backup material for other sources, such
s the civil register, or as a jumping-off point to other
ources. For example, the age of the eldest child of a fam-
ly, as indicated by the census enumerator, might give a
ough indication of the likely date of the marriage of the
arents, which could lead the searcher to consult the rel-
vant marriage indexes. Also, if an ancestor were to disap-
ear from one census to the next it would be reasonable to
ssume that he or she might be dead and useful to consult
he relevant death indexes at St Catherine's House. Of
ourse, he or she might have emigrated or simply been left
ut of the census by accident.

Parish registers

So far we have dealt with only genealogical information
elating to the years following the beginning of civil regis-
ration in 1837 and to those following the beginning of
census-taking in 1841. Obviously, the amateur family his-
orian will want to find out about earlier ancestors. Earlier
information can be had from the parish registers. They
also provide later information, and in the case of a family
the members of which have remained in the same district
for a long time, a family researcher might find it quicker
and cheaper to use the parish register records rather than
the civil registration records at St Catherine's House.

Up until 1813, when the registers of the Church of England were standardized, parish records can be quite diffi-

cult to use and can cause some confusion. A little background knowledge is useful. England and Wales had around 11,000 parishes, differing quite considerably in extent, the largest of these being divided into chapelries or chapels-at-ease. Many of these chapelries were given the right to hold their own baptisms, and marriage and burial services. Sometimes the chapelries kept their own records of these in a separate register, and sometimes the information was recorded in the main parish register, often in a separate section. The family history researcher will find it useful to consult *Guide to the Local Administrative Units of England* by F. A. Youngs.

Parish registration of baptisms, marriages, and burials began in 1538, although very few parishes have records that go so far back, and at first these were recorded on sheets of paper in a fairly unsystematic way, and so many of them have been lost or destroyed. In 1597 a rule was made that the entries of baptism, marriage and burial should be kept in a special register, which should also contain any previous extant records going back to 1538, although some ministers thought that the new ruling extended back only as far as 1558, the year that Elizabeth Tudor came to the throne. Thus it is common to find that most surviving registers relate to years after 1558.

The 1597 ruling also decreed that in future a copy of baptisms, marriages and burials registered during the year should be sent to the bishop's house. These are called bishop's transcripts and are kept at the archives offices of the ancient dioceses, e.g. York and Lincoln, which are dif ferent from the new dioceses created in the late nineteenth and twentieth centuries. These, when they are extant, are extremely useful as substitutes for the original where this has been lost or where it has been rendered illegible. Unfortunately, however, the bishop's transcripts, at least in the earlier years, are even less well preserved than the original parish registers.

One of the major problems with using parish registers is that they are difficult to locate. This is not really surprising, given the length of time involved, given the number and differences in extent of the parishes and given the changes that there have been with the passage of time.

In England and Wales the local record office will most likely be able to help. In 1979 a ruling was made that all parishes should deposit their registers at the local record offices unless the relevant parish could prove that it could satisfactorily store and preserve the registers in good condition. Only a few parish records are now stored in parish churches, and even before the ruling of 1979 some parishes had voluntarily deposited their records in the local record offices because they either did not have the space or the facilities to store the registers themselves. In Scotland the parish registers are stored in Register House.

It is worth checking at the local reference library to see if the parish register that you are seeking is in print. Several parish registers were printed, either privately or by a parish register society. Such societies can be up to a hundred years old, and some of them have several publications in print. If, in fact, the relevant parish register is not in print, you should visit the relevant record office where the registers are usually available for research on microfilm, as are the bishop's transcripts at the ancient diocesan offices. The originals are not usually available because they are old and fragile and would deteriorate badly with a lot of handling.

Another source of information that family historians should think of consulting is the International Genealogical Index, computerized records prepared by the Mormon Church, or The Church of Jesus Christ of the Latter-Day Saints. They are interested in this kind of information because the Mormon Church's members have to trace their ancestors in order that they may be baptised by proxy, but the International Genealogical Index is available to be consulted by anyone, whether or not he or she is a member of the Mormon Church. The Index is available free of charge or for a voluntary donation in specially constructed buildings in various places throughout the country. Microfilm copies of the IGI are also available at some reference libraries and record offices, and the library catalogues of the Mormon's Family History Library are available on CD-ROM.

As with all research sources, there are some words of warning to be considered with reference to the International Genealogical Index, or IGI as it is commonly known. For one thing the index is far from being complete. This is partly because the sheer scale of the material is such that it is bound to take a long time to complete the consolidation of it. It is also partly because some Church of England clerics are unwilling to be involved in such a system because of their objections to people being baptised by proxy into the Mormon church when they had already been baptised by their parents into the Anglican faith. A point also worth remembering is that much of the material for the IGI has been collected by amateurs, who, although interested and enthusiastic, have no specialist training. All this does not detract from the fact, however, that the IGI can save the family researcher a lot of time that would otherwise be spent in consulting parish records directly.

A few points about parish register entries generally may prove helpful to the family researcher. The information given is likely to be sparse. For example, the baptism record may give just the date of the baptism, the name of the child, and the name of the father.

The old custom of starting the official year on 25 March (Lady Day), rather than on 1 January, can cause confusion. Dates relating to baptisms, marriages and burials that occurred between 1 January and 25 March, therefore, may require to have another year added to them. This method of dating records was changed on 1 January 1752, the year that Britain abandoned the Julian calendar in favour of the Gregorian calendar used by the rest of Europe.

It is sometimes forgotten by researchers that parish baptism registers do not record the actual date of birth but the date of the church ceremony at which the child was baptised into the church. The difference between birth and baptism was not usually great, usually a matter of three days or so, but the interval varied from time to time and from place to place.

With reference to marriage registers, most marriage services were performed after the calling of banns in the church, but a number of marriages were performed by licence. Licences were usually issued through diocesan consistory courts and were recorded in the bishop's register.

The Marriage Act of 1753 tried to standardize the form of entry for marriage in the parish register. In the light of a concern to prevent illegal marriages, this Act stated that every marriage must be preceded by the calling of the banns or the issue of a licence, that the marriage ceremony must be performed in the parish of which either the bride or the groom was a resident, and that a record of the marriage must be kept in a book specially assigned for the purpose. It further legislated for the fact that henceforth entries in the marriage register had to be signed by the bride and the groom and by witnesses in a bound volume of printed forms. In 1836 civil ceremonies conducted by a registrar were allowed.

An Act passed in 1812 but coming into effect on 1 January 1813 sought to standardize the Church of England parish registers. From then on the parish registers consist of bound volumes of printed forms and are easier to use, and provide more information. Under the terms of the Act of 1812, an entry in the baptismal register gives the name of the child, the date of baptism, the forenames and surname of the parents, the place of residence of the parents, and the occupation of the father. An entry in the marriage register notes the names of the bride and the groom, the respective parishes in which they lived, and the occupation of the father. An entry in the burial register gives the name of the deceased, the place of residence of the deceased, the date of burial, and the age of the deceased.

There is the possibility of error in parish registers. For example, the family researcher may find a tombstone in the churchyard but also find that there is no corresponding entry in the parish burial register. One possible explanation is carelessness on the part of the keeper of the register. However, for at least the three centuries that preceded compulsory civil registration, the parish registers are essential. In addition, if the members of the family who are the subjects of the researcher's quest lived for a great deal of time in rather a restricted area of the country in the nineteenth century and were members of the Church of England, then the relevant parish registers will save a great deal of searching in the civil registers in St Catherine's House.

Other sources

Other records are also helpful to the family historian in the search for family roots. These include trade and commercial directories, a collection of which may well be found in a reasonably large, well-equipped reference library. The drawback with these is that they are far from comprehensive since they have a tendency to concentrate on craftsmen, tradesmen and professional people in an area and ignore those who were unskilled workers, such as labourers or servants.

It may also be worth checking probate records, although many people did not bother making wills for various reasons. First, will-making was very much the preserve of the well-off—those who had nothing to leave were obviously not much worried about making wills. Second, it had often been made quite clear by the deceased when he was alive—and no one thought to challenge this when he was dead—what was to happen to any property or money on his death—for example, the eldest son might inherit the land and younger siblings get a share of the money. Third, as is indeed still the case, many people simply did not bother making a will or never got round to it. Fourth, married women rarely bothered to make wills, since they could do nothing without the consent of their husbands, although some widows and unmarried women made wills.

Until 1858 it was the responsibility of the church to prove a will, and so probate records up till then are held at the ancient diocesan record offices. In 1858 the state took over from the church the responsibility for proving wills, either through district offices throughout the country or through the Principal Registry in London, from 1874 housed at Somerset House in the Strand. The Principal Registry also holds copies of wills that have been proved in the district offices. This applies to England and Wales.

The annual indexes of probates for the whole of England and Wales are available for consultation in the Principal Registry, and some of the larger municipal libraries throughout the country have printed copies available. In the indexes you will find the name of the person who made the will—the testator—his or her address, the date of death, sometimes the place of death, the date of probate, the names of the executors or administrators, the total value of the testator's estate, and the name of the office where the will was proved.

Another useful source of information for the family researcher, at least in respect of male members of the family, might be military records. Information about men who served in the armed forces can be obtained at the General Register Office at St Catherine's House, London, and the Public Record Office at Kew. It is obviously extremely useful and timesaving if the name of the regiment is known.

Throughout the centuries men were expected to present themselves for active service in the militia when occasion demanded. Lists of names of men liable for service, known as muster rolls or militia returns, were drawn up periodically from the sixteenth century to the nineteenth century. The muster rolls relating to Tudor and Stuart times are kept in the old Public Record Office at Chancery Lane in London, with some being held in local record offices. A book that will prove useful to someone wishing to consult these is *Tudor and Stuart Muster Rolls: A Directory of Holdings in the British Isles* by Jeremy Gibson and Alan Dell. Another useful book is *Militia Lists and Musters, 1757-1876: A Directory of Holdings in the British Isles* by Jeremy Gibson and Mervyn Medlycot.

There are still more sources, but the embryo family re-searcher has more than enough in this chapter to get quite far along the way to establishing a family tree. It has been mentioned earlier in the chapter that some people are ben-efiting from recent technology by using home computers in the compilation of their family trees and by the fact that the library catalogues of the Mormon's Family History Library are on CD-ROM.

Others are likely to benefit from even more recent tech-nology. The Internet, by giving instant access to global in-formation, is likely to prove a great boon, particularly for those seeking information on foreign ancestors. There are already hundreds of genealogical files on the Internet, and the number is certain to increase greatly. As the range of historical information on the Internet increases, so will the Internet practically revolutionize the task of someone wishing to know more about his or her family history.

By whatever means they go about their research, family historians are likely to find the whole task utterly absorb-ing. Furthermore, by learning about their ancestors and about the various branches of the family they will come to a much clearer understanding of how they became the people they are today. For some this will be a welcome bonus, for others it will prove an important point in their attempt to get more in touch with their inner selves, a valuable stage in their journey of self-discovery, although one with its roots in the past.